EMT Study Guide Complete A-Z Review By

Jamie Montoya

Table Of Contents

Intro	8
Overview	10
Section 1: Airway, Respiration, and Ventilation	11
Section 2: Cardiology and Resuscitation	11
Section 3: EMS Operations	12
Section 4: Medical and Obstetrics/Gynecology	13
Section 5: Trauma	14
Section 1: Airway, Respiration, and Ventilation	15
Part 1: Anatomy of the Respiratory System	16
Part 2: Physiology of the respiratory System	19
Part 3: Respiration Pathophysiology	25
Part 4: Respiratory Assessment	30
Part 5: Opening, Clearing, and Maintaining the Airway	33
Part 6: Supplemental Oxygen, Assisted Ventilation, and Special Conditions	39

Part 7: Respiratory Emergencies and Respiratory Conditions	46
Section 2: Cardiology and Resuscitation	**56**
Part 1: Cardiac Anatomy and Physiology	57
Part 2: Cardiac Pathophysiology	62
Part 3: Patient Assessment in Event of a Cardiac Emergency	72
Part 4: Chest Pain or Discomfort, Cardiac Monitoring, and Age Concerns	82
Part 5: Cardiac Assistive Devices and Defibrillators	90
Part 6: AED or Automated External Defibrillator	95
Part 7: Cardiac Arrest Care	102
Part 8: CPR (Cardiopulmonary Resuscitation)	106
Part 9: Airway Obstructions	112
Part 10: Circulation Assist Devices	116
Part 11: Special Conditions and Ongoing Education	119
Section 3: EMS Operations	**123**
Part 1: EMS Systems	123
Part 2: Workforce Safety and Wellness	134
Part 3: Legal, Medical, and Ethical Issues	141
Part 4: Documentation and Communication	152

Part 5: Patient Assessment	159
Part 6: Lifting and Moving Patients	165
Part 7: Transport Operations	172
Part 8: Team Cooperation	177
Part 9: Incident Management	181
Part 10: Vehicle Extrication and Special Rescue	185
Part 11: Terrorism and Disaster Response and Management	188
Section 4: Medical and Obstetrics/Gynecology	194
Part 1: Types of Medical Emergencies and Common Treatment	195
Part 2: Medical Terminology	201
Part 3: The Human Body	204
Part 4: LifeSpan Development	214
Part 5: Neurologic Emergencies	217
Part 6: Gastrointestinal and Urologic Emergencies	223
Part 7: Endocrine and Hematologic Emergencies	225
Part 8: Immunologic Emergencies	229
Part 9: Pharmacology	232
Part 10: Toxicology	234

Part 11: Psychiatric Emergencies	237
Part 12: Gynecological Emergencies	241
Part 13: Obstetrics and Neonatal Care	244
Part 14: Pediatric Emergencies	252
Part 15: Geriatric Emergencies	260
Section 5: Trauma	267
Part 1: Trauma Basics	269
Part 2: Soft Tissue Injuries	282
Part 3: Neck and Facial Injuries	290
Part 4: Head and Spinal Injuries	296
Part 5: Chest Injuries	304
Part 6: Abdominal and Genitourinary Injuries	310
Part 7: Orthopedic Injuries	318
Part 8: Environmental Emergencies	324
Part 9: Shock	332

EMT Study Guide Complete A-Z Review for the EMT Exam

Intro

Welcome to the EMT Study Guide and Review for the EMT Exam. The EMT exam draws from the entire range of current medical knowledge. It is intended to review your understanding of all the information and procedures necessary to save lives in the various emergency situations that you will encounter in the field as an Emergency Medical Technician. Because of this, it is impossible to predict the full range of subjects and details you will encounter on the exam. However, this review divides the whole of medical knowledge pertinent to emergency medical services into five different sections, each emphasized proportionally to the knowledge you will need for the test and in the field.

Three of the sections in this study guide address particular types of challenges faced by EMTs in the field: issues with airway, respiration and ventilation, cardiology and resuscitation, and trauma. One section relates to special conditions which pertain to certain patients: a variety of specific concerns regarding obstetrics and gynecology, geriatrics, infant care, and special medical conditions. One section refers to EMS operations, including the scope of duties of EMT's, as well as that of BLS, ALS, and paramedics.

The section on airway, respiration, and ventilation is the first area addressed, as blockages in the airway and other respiratory system disruptions can be more immediately life-threatening than any other condition. The second section addresses cardiology and resuscitation, as this is the second most essential system required to stabilize a patient. Following this, the third section explores EMS operations and the scope of work required from the EMT in the performance of his or her duties. Section 4 explores medical conditions, geriatrics, OB/GYN considerations, infant care, and other patient-specific concerns. In the final section, trauma is addressed. The EMT must be prepared to face a wide range of different traumas in the course of medical services, and handling trauma effectively requires an in-depth knowledge of anatomy, physiology, and treatment procedures.

Please note that this guide is intended to supplement, not replace, the information covered in your EMT classes. The EMT exam itself is not designed to test a single set curriculum, but rather to explore the current range of medical knowledge necessary for the proper function of the EMT. Remember, the goal itself is not to simply pass an exam, but to ensure that you are fully prepared to enter the Emergency Medical Services as an EMT. This information is intended to aid you in saving lives, and it is vital that it be known and understood thoroughly. Therefore, take note of any areas where you feel a bit vague, and use them as indications of where the material should be studied more intensively.

Let's begin with a brief overview of the material covered in each section:

Overview

Section 1: Airway, Respiration, and Ventilation

The EMT exam will explore your knowledge concerning the breathing process. This includes the anatomy involved, such as the parts of the body that facilitate breathing that make up the respiratory system. It also includes the physiological aspects of respiration, such as ventilation and oxygenation. Also included are the equipment and techniques used by the EMT to restore breathing or ease the process in the event of medical emergencies. This is important as unrelated emergencies can have respiratory complications, and these must be addressed prior to other medical treatment. Section 1 offers a brief synopsis of the information needed for an EMT to handle respiratory issues.

Section 2: Cardiology and Resuscitation

Proper blood flow and heart function is necessary for survival for more than a few minutes, so it is necessary for an EMT to be prepared for cardiac emergencies. The circulatory system is complex and extends throughout the entire body. Because of this, it is essential to have an in-depth understanding of the whole system and all parts of the body involved. Issues with the heart and the function of the heart can arise in times of emergency, and responding appropriately to these problems in the first few minutes of an emergency can mean the difference between the life and death of a patient. This section highlights the information necessary for the EMT to handle these problems effectively.

Section 3: EMS Operations

The EMT is one element of the EMS service, a coordinated system of facilities and personnel dedicated to responding to emergencies and saving lives. In order for the EMT to function most effectively, he or she must understand the role they play in this interconnected system. Each element of the system is subject to specific procedures and guidelines, helping the whole service to operate in a smoothly coordinated fashion. This section explores the different elements of the EMS system. It also explores the responsibilities and guidelines which give the scope and function of the EMT within the EMS system.

Section 4: Medical and Obstetrics/Gynecology

In addition, to cardiac and airway emergencies, there are a range of other conditions which require the attention of Emergency Medical Services. An EMT must be prepared to handle anything from seizure to loss of consciousness, overdose, unexpected childbirth, poisoning, and a range of other emergencies. To top it off, often the exact condition is unknown when the EMT first arrives on the scene. Therefore, it is essential to know the proper methods for assessing a patient quickly and effectively so that life-saving medical attention can be provided without delay.

Finally, each patient has their own unique needs. One cannot handle an adult in the same way that they would an infant or a geriatric patient. There are also a range of concerns which require a basic knowledge of obstetrics and gynecology. This section explores the various medical conditions which an EMT may encounter in the line of their duty and the adjustments necessary when treating patients with specific concerns.

Section 5: Trauma

In the final section, we will deal with trauma. Trauma can be in the form of accident or injury to any part of the body. Alternately, it can be in the form of emotional shock. The EMT must be prepared to handle a wide range of possible medical emergencies. Physical injury can occur in many ways to every part of the body and each type of injury must be handled differently. Proper treatment requires a comprehensive understanding of basic anatomy and physiology as well as a familiarity with many specialized procedures for dealing with specific injuries. In addition, the EMT must have a strong grasp of medical terminology to effectively express medical conditions to doctors, paramedics, and other health care professionals.

Finally, emotional trauma can be just as challenging as physical trauma. The EMT must be prepared to handle patients in a delicate emotional state, helping to stabilize them until they can receive more specialized care. The section on trauma explores the entire range of different concerns regarding physical and emotional trauma.

Section 1: Airway, Respiration, and Ventilation

Oxygen is the most vital need of the body, and of each cell within the body. We fulfill this need by breathing, by exchanging carbon dioxide with fresh oxygen. The respiratory system is the collection of organs which facilitate the process of breathing and oxygenation. This section covers the anatomy and physiology of the respiratory system as well as respiratory pathophysiology, or the numerous problems that can interrupt proper respiratory function.

Also in this section are areas which address how to assess patients for respiratory complications and address specific concerns, and how to manage the airway for individual patients. Techniques for opening and maintaining the airway are reviewed, both with and without equipment. In addition, this section covers assisted ventilation and supplemental oxygen, as well as common respiratory emergencies, recommended treatment for common emergencies, and special respiratory conditions.

Part 1: Anatomy of the Respiratory System

The respiratory system is composed of two portions: the upper airway and lower airway. Each of these plays an essential role in the breathing process, and each is composed of other specialized structures. The upper airway includes the nose and mouth (collectively referred to as the oral cavity), as well as the jaw, tongue, larynx, and pharynx. The pharynx is seated above the larynx and is the membrane-lined cavity behind the nose and mouth. The upper portion of the pharynx, the portion which is seated above and behind the soft palate and directly connected to the nasal cavity, is termed the nasopharynx.

The larynx is a hollow muscular organ which holds the vocal cords and forms an air passage to the lungs. It is seated directly above the trachea. The larynx is protected by the thyroid cartilage, a portion of cartilage that wraps the central portion of the throat and forms the Adam's apple. The upper airway warms and moistens air prior to entry into the lungs. It serves as the pathway for air into and out of the lungs. When dealing with foreign bodies which obstruct breathing, it is the upper airway which must be cleared or circumvented.

The lower airway is the portion of the respiratory system which consists of the lungs, bronchi, and trachea. The trachea is a membranous tube lined with rings of cartilage which leads from the larynx to the right and left bronchi. The trachea is wrapped by a structure known as the cricoid cartilage. The cricoid cartilage is seated directly below the thyroid cartilage. It forms the dorsal portion of the larynx and then wraps ventrally around the sides of the trachea, thinning as it moves to the front of the throat. The cricoid cartilage and thyroid cartilage are joined by the cricothyroid membrane, a membrane of yellow elastic tissue which connects dorsally to the arytenoid cartilages.

The bronchi lead from the trachea to the right and left lung. Each of the lungs is divided into lobes. The right lung contains three lobes: the lower, middle, and upper. The left lung contains only two lobes, the upper and lower. Each of these lobes is further divided into millions of tiny membranous sacs termed alveoli. The alveoli are the site of gas exchange. They are wrapped by capillaries which receive oxygen into hemoglobin molecules in the blood after inhalation and release carbon dioxide into the contained air in the alveoli prior to exhalation. Epithelial cells in the alveoli are also responsible for secreting respiratory surfactant. This is a substance composed of proteins and lipids which reduces surface tension at the air-liquid interface within the lungs. This contributes to the elasticity of pulmonary tissue, prevents the alveoli from collapsing, and makes breathing easier.

It is important to remember that differences exist between the airway of an adult and that of a child. First, the child's lower and upper airways, including trachea, mouth, and nose, are smaller than those of the adult. This smaller size means that it is more likely for the child's airway to be obstructed. At the same time, the child's upper and lower airways are more flexible. Finally, the tongue of a child is proportionally larger than that of the adult. Because of this, the tongue can more easily block the airway.

Part 2: Physiology of the respiratory System

There are two processes involved in the physiology of the respiratory system: ventilation and respiration. The function of the respiratory system is oxygenation, or the addition of oxygen to the body. The site of oxygenation is the lungs. Oxygen from the air drawn into the lungs is exchanged with carbon dioxide in the blood. Oxygenated blood then flows throughout the body to deliver oxygen to all cells and tissues. The processes of ventilation and respiration are involuntary. In other words, they occur reflexively, without the need for thought or intention.

The first phase of the respiratory process, ventilation, is what we commonly call breathing. Breathing is the contraction and expansion of the thoracic cavity to bring air into and push air out of the lungs. The muscular action that drives "quiet" breathing, or breathing during the resting state, comes from the diaphragm and intercostal muscles. In times of extreme exertion or in the case of some respiratory dysfunctions, accessory muscles such as the scalene and sternocleidomastoid are recruited to further expand the thoracic cavity. The lungs expand when the intercostal muscles and diaphragm contract. As the lungs expand, the pressure of the air within the lungs drops. The pressure gradient causes air to be pulled into the lungs, causing air to be inhaled. As the intercostal muscles and diaphragm relax, the thoracic cavity and lungs contract. This raises the pressure of air within the lungs forcing air out in the process of exhalation.

In healthy individuals, the process of breathing or ventilation occurs with minimal effort. However, when a patient is experiencing dyspnea, labored or difficult breathing, it is an indication that their unassisted ventilation is not sufficient to oxygenate their system. In these instances, it may be necessary to provide assisted ventilation. Assisted ventilation will improve a patient's tidal flow, the amount of air moved into and out of their lungs while breathing. This will bring more oxygen-rich air into the lungs, and thus, more oxygen into the bloodstream.

Atmospheric air is a combination of gases, including oxygen, nitrogen, water vapor, and trace amounts of other elements. A combined gas will exert a total pressure on the walls of its container. This total pressure is the sum of the partial pressures of all of the gases which composes it. The partial pressure is proportional to the percentage of an individual gas out of the total volume of combined gases. As air enters the alveoli of the lungs, it exerts pressure on the alveolar membranes, the sites of oxygen transfer into the blood. The amount of oxygen available is related to the partial pressure of oxygen; put another way, as the partial pressure of oxygen increases, more oxygen can be absorbed into the blood. Another consideration is that air drawn through the upper airway is humidified. Water vapor is added to the total volume, reducing the partial pressure of oxygen in the lungs relative to atmospheric conditions.

The involuntary breathing reflex is triggered in healthy patients by an increase of carbon dioxide in the bloodstream. This increase is detected by chemoreceptors, cells in the nervous system that register the presence of chemicals. In some instances, though, a respiratory dysfunction can result in chronically high carbon dioxide levels in the bloodstream. COPD is one common example of such a condition. Patients with chronically elevated levels of carbon dioxide become adjusted to these levels. Their system then triggers ventilation on the basis of decreased oxygen levels rather than carbon dioxide. This condition is termed hypoxic drive.

Ventilation facilitates oxygenation. Oxygenation is the absorption of oxygen into the bloodstream and body. Once the alveoli are filled with air, gas exchange occurs between the carbon dioxide in the blood and the oxygen within the air. Oxygen is necessary for the proper function of all tissues and organs. Even when ventilation is operating without disruption, oxygenation can be disrupted in various ways. Oxygenation can be insufficient when the air has low levels of oxygen. This can happen in confined spaces with limited amounts of air. It can also occur in high altitudes. At higher elevations, the percentage of oxygen in the air is significantly lower than in lower altitudes. In addition to these environmental causes, there are a range of physiological conditions which can result in insufficient oxygen intake.

When a patient does not absorb adequate levels of oxygen into the bloodstream, they will enter a state of hypoxia. Symptoms of this condition include confusion, followed by tachypnea, or abnormal rapidness of breath, and finally cyanosis. Cyanosis is a bluish cast to skin and mucous membranes, beginning peripherally and spreading as the state of hypoxia becomes more severe. A patient can be tested for mild hypoxia by pressing firmly on a nail tip for a few seconds and then releasing pressure. In healthy patients, the pinkish color will return very quickly, within a couple of seconds. However, if the color of the flesh beneath the nail remains white for longer than this, the patient is poorly oxygenated. If the mucus membranes and extremities exhibit extreme cyanosis, the lack of oxygenation is serious enough to cause profound health complications.

The ventilation or breathing process carries oxygen into the lungs. This oxygen must then be absorbed by the hemoglobin in the blood and delivered throughout the cells and tissues of the body. The delivery of oxygen to all cells and tissues is termed respiration. There are two phases of respiration: external and internal. The first step in the process is external respiration. This is the movement of oxygen and carbon dioxide across the alveolar walls. Carbon dioxide is released from the hemoglobin molecules into the alveolar spaces. Simultaneously, oxygen is absorbed from the alveolar spaces into the hemoglobin molecules.

After this occurs, the blood travels throughout the body suffusing all tissues and cells. The cells absorb oxygen from the blood and release carbon dioxide into it. This is termed internal respiration. Diffusion drives both external and internal respiration, causing oxygen to move along the concentration gradient from higher to lower concentrations.

Aside from external and internal respiration, there is one more type – cellular respiration. Cellular respiration is the processing of oxygen and sugars within the cells which produces energy in the form of ATP. All of the physiological processes of our cells and tissues are dependent upon this steady production of energy for proper function, and thus, for survival of the organism. This is why lack of oxygenation to the system, even for a short amount of time, can cause severe damage or death.

Part 3: Respiration Pathophysiology

Given the complexity of the respiration process, there are a number of ways that it can be disrupted. Problems with any part of the anatomy of the respiratory system itself can cause poor oxygenation. In addition, the nervous system, circulatory system, and respiratory system coordinate to facilitate respiration. If the interaction between these systems is lacking, then the patient will not receive sufficient oxygenation.

The nervous system is vital for stimulating the breathing reflex. The respiratory centers of the brain in the medulla oblongata and pons trigger the rate and depth of breathing motions in the diaphragm and intercostal muscles. The nervous system receives signals from chemoreceptors, sensory cells that respond to chemical stimuli. These chemoreceptors monitor levels of oxygen and carbon dioxide, as well as the pH of the spinal fluid. In healthy individuals, high carbon dioxide and low pH will cause an increase in the rate or depth of breath. When the nervous system is compromised, the breathing reflex can be interrupted. This is one condition which can result in hypercapnia, or an excess of carbon dioxide in the blood.

There are a number of pulmonary factors which can also interfere with ventilation. Extrinsic factors, or those which come from outside the body, include airway obstructions due to foreign bodies or physical trauma that interferes with the ventilation process. A number of intrinsic factors can also disrupt ventilation. Intrinsic factors can be in the form of allergic reactions or infections of the lung. They can also include airflow blockage if the tongue obstructs the air passage or the tissues of the airway swell and become constricted.

Even if ventilation itself is adequate, there are some conditions which can cause poor oxygenation. One instance of such a condition is a mismatch between ventilation and perfusion. Perfusion refers to the amount of blood going to the lungs. The amount of blood which goes to the lungs must be matched with the amount of ventilation for sufficient gas exchange. The balance between ventilation and perfusion is termed the ventilation/perfusion ratio. If the lungs receive insufficient blood flow, then normal ventilation rates will not be able to sufficiently oxygenation the blood.

Another example of mismatched ventilation/perfusion ratios is the case of intrapulmonary shunting. When the blood flow to the alveoli is normal, but no air is able to reach a certain region of the lung, then the ventilation/perfusion ratio for that part of the lung is zero. Regardless of the levels of ventilation of other regions or the blood flow to the alveoli, the affected region of the lung is not participating in oxygenation.

Disruptions can also occur in the respiration part of the process. Again, respiration is the transfer of oxygen across the alveolar membrane and into the hemoglobin molecules in the blood, as well as the spread of oxygen from the blood throughout all tissues and cells in the body. Respiration can be disrupted externally by altitude or other external conditions where the partial pressure of oxygen is lower than that required for sufficient oxygenation. Excess carbon monoxide in the environment can also interfere with respiration externally by binding to the hemoglobin molecules.

Internal factors can also disrupt respiration by reducing the surface area of the lung which serves gas exchange. Lung infections can block off areas of the lung and make them inaccessible to air. COPD, or chronic obstructive pulmonary disease, is another internal disruption to respiration. COPD is a blanket term which includes a range of diseases – including emphysema and chronic bronchitis – which block the exchange of air into the lungs. Another condition which internally interferes with respiration is pulmonary edema. In this condition, fluid collects in the lungs as a result of pneumonia, trauma, or toxins. Emergency treatment for these conditions generally requires supplemental oxygen.

Issues with the circulatory system can also interfere with the respiration process. Several conditions can interrupt blood flow and decrease oxygenation at the tissue level. A pulmonary embolism is a blood clot in a pulmonary artery that interferes with the blood reaching the lungs. Another condition is tension pneumothorax, a progressive buildup of air in the pleural space surrounding the lungs. This causes a compression of the lung and obstructs venous return. One way to treat tension pneumothorax in emergency situations is to create positive pressure ventilation to relieve pressure. In other words, a chest tube can be inserted into the pleural space to relieve pressure. A number of traumatic injuries can interrupt the flow of blood to the tissues. Finally, cardiac problems can prevent the heart from delivering oxygen-rich blood to the tissues and organs.

Part 4: Respiratory Assessment

One of the first steps for the EMT when they arrive on the scene is to assess the patient's breathing. There are several factors to this assessment, including whether the breathing is abnormal or adequate, whether the patient is sufficiently oxygenated, and whether the airway is open or closed. If the patient is breathing, assess the respiratory rate and work of breathing. A Normal respiratory rate for an adult is 12-20 breaths per minute. For children ages 6-11 the normal respiratory rate is 18-25 breaths per minute. It is also necessary to assess a patient's level of consciousness, as this will be impacted if respiration is insufficient. All abnormal signs like labored breath or abnormally fast or slow breathing are potential indicators of a condition which impacts the respiratory system.

Work of breathing is the energy required to inhale and exhale. It increases with increased airway resistance or reduced thoracic or lung compliance. Labored breathing is a visible indicator of abnormally increased work of breathing. In some instances, retractions will be observed in a patient working very hard to breath. A retraction is when the area between ribs and neck sink in when the patient is trying to inhale. This is often observed in patients with severe asthma. Agonal gasps are another abnormal breathing pattern characterized by gasping, labored breaths, odd vocalizations, and myoclonus, or spasmodic muscle contractions. Agonal gasps can be caused by cardiac arrest or cerebral ischemia, a reduced flow of blood to the brain, among other factors.

Irregular breathing is another potential sign of health conditions. There are certain characteristic irregular breathing patterns. One such pattern is termed ataxic respiration. Ataxic respiration is completely irregular breathing punctuated by periods of apnea, or cessation of breath. A characteristic form of ataxic respiration is Cheyne-Stokes respiration, a pattern in which breathing deepens progressively, and occasionally becomes progressively more rapid as well, punctuated by periods of apnea. This pattern repeats in a cycle taking from 30 seconds to two minutes. Cheyne-Stokes respiration is often exhibited in patients with heart failure or stroke.

Oxygenation levels are another aspect of respiratory assessment. Low oxygenation can occur even with adequate ventilation, if gas exchange is inadequate. In emergency situations, oxygenation levels can be assessed with a finger pulse oximeter. Pulse oximetry measures both heart rate and changes in blood oxygen level. Normal pulse oximeter readings range from 95-100 percent. Prior to the use of the pulse oximeter, the EMT can assess level of consciousness and the presence of cyanosis, or bluing to the skin, lips, and nails. Low oxygen levels in the blood can be indicative of COPD, congestive heart failure, asthma, and a range of other conditions.

Hypoxia can also be assessed through capnography, which measures the concentration of carbon dioxide in exhaled gases. This is known as end tidal CO2. Elevated end tidal CO2 can be indicative of hypoventilation or increased metabolic activity, while low end tidal CO2 can indicate low pulmonary perfusion or decreased cardiac output, both of which are potential indicators of shock.

Part 5: Opening, Clearing, and Maintaining the Airway

If the patient is not breathing or unresponsive, the first step is to check the airway to ensure that it is and remains open. One common issue with unconscious patients is the obstruction of the airway by the tongue. There are several maneuvers with which the EMT should be familiar to prevent this from happening. The first step for all of these maneuvers is to place the patient in a supine position, if this is possible in the situation and given the patient's condition. Next, assess the patient's condition to determine the appropriate maneuver. Further injury can result if the inappropriate technique is chosen.

The first technique and most preferred is the head tilt-chin lift. This maneuver involves lightly pressing down on the forehead to tilt the head backwards while lifting the lower part of the face from just below the point of the chin. This places the patient in the "sniffing position", the ideal position for intubation and manual ventilation. However, this technique involves significant flexion of the neck and should be avoided if there is the possibility of injury in the cervical spine.

In the case of suspected neck or cervical spine injury, the jaw-thrust is the preferred maneuver for opening the airway. The aim is to move the jaw forwards with minimal neck motion. From above the patient's head, place the index and middle fingers of both hands behind the posterior angles of the jaw. Gently lift, bringing the mandible forward to open the airway by lowering the tongue away from the pharynx. Place the thumbs on the chin and press down lightly but firmly to open the mouth. This will displace the mandible forward, pulling the tongue down and preventing it from obstructing the airway. The jaw lift is contraindicated if the patient has suffered severe facial injury.

In some instances, the mouth will not open with the head tilt-chin lift or the jaw-thrust alone. In this case, it may be necessary to open the mouth manually. This is done by placing the thumb on the lower teeth and the index finger on the upper teeth. Gently press the lower teeth down and the upper teeth up. This will allow you to visualize the oropharynx, or the portion of the pharynx at the back of the oral cavity. All three maneuvers can be combined to maximize the opening of the airway. This is known as the triple airway maneuver. Place fingers behind the point of the jaw, base of the hands on the forehead, and thumbs on the chin. Tile the head backwards and lift the jaw by lifting with the fingers and pressing with the base of the hands. At the same time, use the thumbs to press the chin down to open the mouth.

If none of these maneuvers is suitable for the patient, they can be turned laterally as a basic form of airway management. This involves placing the patient in the recovery position. To do this, roll the body to one side. Extend the lower arm and place the upper hand beneath the cheek. By turning the patient laterally, the tongue is prevented from obstructing the airway. This also decreases the potential of aspiration in the event that the patient vomits. This is a simple and effective way to maintain the airway. However, it is contraindicated if the patient is suspected of having a spinal injury.

After the head lift-chin thrust or jaw-thrust maneuvers, it may be necessary to suction secretions from the patient's airway. Vomit, blood, or mucus may block the passage of air.

This will be obvious if the patient is gurgling or if you see large amounts of blood or vomit. In the process of intubation, it will be necessary to visualize the vocal cords before inserting the tube. Suctioning will be required prior to insertion if the vocal cords are not already visible.

Suctioning can be accomplished with a portable device or with a fixed unit mounted inside of an ambulance. Prior to suctioning, the device should be fitted with a catheter suitable for the patient's needs and the given operation. Flexible-tipped catheters, also known as French catheters, are suitable for suctioning the trachea or nose. Rigid-tipped catheters, also known as Yankauers, are suitable for suctioning the mouth.

To suction the airway clear, gather the necessary materials and add the desired catheter tip to the vacuum device. Turn the device on and set the pressure at 300 mmHg. If suctioning the mouth, insert the tip of the catheter into the mouth only as far as you can see. Apply suction while withdrawing the catheter. Suction time should be limited to 15 seconds for adults. If treating children, then the suction time should be limited to 10 seconds.

In some instances, the patient's airway must be kept open with airway adjuncts. An airway adjunct keeps the mouth open and prevents the tongue from obstructing the airway. Prior to inserting an airway adjunct, it is necessary to assess the patient. Assessment is essential to determine the patient's level of consciousness. It will also help you to determine the appropriate size of airway adjunct and whether an oropharyngeal or nasopharyngeal adjunct should be used.

Oropharyngeal airway adjuncts are inserted through the mouth and into the pharynx. An oropharyngeal airway is only suitable if the patient is unresponsive and lacks an intact gag reflex. It can be used for both patients that require manual ventilation and those that are breathing normally. If the patient's gag reflex is intact, then the nasopharyngeal airway adjunct is recommended. This adjunct is led through the nose and into the pharynx. It is suitable for patients with altered levels of consciousness who are unable to maintain their airway without assistance.

Part 6: Supplemental Oxygen, Assisted Ventilation, and Special Conditions

If the patient is hypoxic, they will require supplemental oxygen. In primary assessment, hypoxic patients will exhibit confusion, a shortness of breath, and cyanosis, or a bluing of the skin and nail beds. Also remember to use supplemental oxygen if a patient requires manual ventilation. Delivery devices for supplemental oxygen come in the form of pressurized-gas cylinders and liquid oxygen. Liquid oxygen is not commonly used in the field, though it may be present in the homes of patients with chronic respiratory conditions.

Oxygen cylinders come in different-sizes. D-size cylinders, which hold 406 liters of oxygen, and M-size cylinders, which hold 3000 liters of oxygen, are those most often used in the field. Cylinders must be fitted with a pressure regulator and flow meter. The pressure regulator is used to reduce the pressure to between 40 and 70 psi. The flow meter is used to dial in a desired flow rate and deliver a steady volume of oxygen per minute. Most modern regulators come with a built-in flow meter. If this is not the case, then the flow regulator should be attached after the regulator.

In order to administer supplemental oxygen, it is first necessary to inspect the cylinder and remove the seal. Crack the cylinder prior to use by using a tank key to open and close the valve. Attach the regulator and flow meter to the tank. The equipment will be fitted with a pin system that permits only one way of assembly. Next, fit the oxygen delivery device onto the nipple of the flow meter or regulator. Oxygen delivery devices come in the form of a nasal cannulas or masks. Set the flow meter to the desired flow rate and administer oxygen to the patient.

It is important to remember that the use of oxygen involves certain hazards. While oxygen does not combust spontaneously, it will combust readily in the presence of spark or flame. It is important to be conscious of the environment. Make sure that oxygen is not used in the presence of a lit cigarette or fireplace. The cylinder should not be left leaning against a wall or standing upright, as a falling cylinder can create sparks. Lay the cylinder down or make sure it is housed in an oxygen cart. The final hazard to consider is the potential of oxygen toxicity. If oxygen levels in the blood become too high, then the patient may experience tissue damage. It is important to keep the flow rate as low as reasonably possible. At the same time, it is critical for patients experiencing hypoxia to receive supplemental oxygen. They should not be deprived of oxygen altogether, nor should the flow rate be set so low that they are insufficiently oxygenated.

Emergency oxygen delivery devices come in four forms: the bag mask, non-rebreather mask, venturi mask, or nasal cannula. Each of these devices delivers a different percentage of oxygen and must be set at a different flow rate. If the patient requires assisted ventilation, then a bag mask should be used. Bag masks can deliver nearly 100% oxygen and the flow rate should be set at 15 liters per minute. Non-rebreather masks can deliver approximately 95% oxygen. The flow rate for non-rebreathers should be set between 10 and 15 liters per minute. Non-rebreathers should be used for potentially hypoxic patients who can breathe without assisted ventilation.

A nasal cannula can deliver between 24 and 44% oxygen and the flow rate should be set between 1 and 6 liters. The nasal cannula is suitable for patients breathing without ventilator assistance who do not tolerate a mask. The venturi mask, also known as an air-entrainment mask, delivers from 24 to 60% oxygen and can be used at flow rates up to 15 liters per minute. Venturi masks deliver a constant rate of oxygen and mix it with the surrounding air. They are helpful to prevent the buildup of excessive carbon dioxide in the blood. Venturi masks are more common for use in long-term care than in the field, as they help prevent COPD patients and others with chronic respiratory ailments from shifting to a hypoxic drive.

It is necessary to assist the patient's ventilation if the patient is experiencing apnea or is unable to ventilate sufficiently on their own power. Passive ventilation can be delivered with chest compressions. Assisted ventilation can be provided manually with a bag valve mask device, or mechanically with CPAP machines or mechanical ventilators. CPAP (Continuous Positive Airway Pressure) machines are suitable only for patients that are breathing spontaneously. They reduce the work of breathing by delivering continuous positive pressure to the lungs. This improves both oxygenation and tidal volumes. BiPAP (Bilevel Positive Airway Pressure) machines function similarly to CPAP, but have an additional features for timing the breath and forcing inhalation if too long has gone between breaths and for reducing pressure during the exhalation phase. Both machines are commonly used for patients with sleep apnea.

Mechanical transport ventilators or bag mask ventilators operate through positive pressure, and both are often used in the field. The benefit of mechanical ventilators over bag-mask devices is that they do not require continuous operator effort. They are often pneumatic-controlled or computer controlled. With all forms of assisted ventilation, the EMT should watch out for gastric distention, which is the tendency for the stomach to bloat as air is blown into it. This occurs when too much air is delivered during assisted ventilation. It is also important to monitor pulmonary compliance during mechanical ventilation. Pulmonary compliance is the lung's capacity to stretch and recoil.

There are a range of special respiratory issues that require specific adaptations to respiratory airway management. One of the most common to encounter in the field is airway obstruction. The airway can be intrinsically obstructed by the swelling of the tissues of the airway or by plugs of mucus. The airway can be obstructed extrinsically by foreign objects. In adults, food is the most common foreign body to block the airway. In children, it is common for other foreign bodies such as toys to become lodged in the pharynx.

Patients with mild or incomplete airway obstructions will exhibit wheezing, weak coughs, and stridor, or an abnormal, high-pitched sound caused by the passage of turbulent airflow past a partial obstruction. Sever or complete airway obstruction results in an inability to speak, cyanosis, and eventually a complete loss of consciousness. In conscious adults and children above one year old, alternate five abdominal thrusts with five back blows until the foreign object is dislodged or the patient becomes unconscious. In conscious infants, back blows should be alternated with chest thrusts, similar to those applied for infant CPR, but sharper and spaced further apart. If patients become unconscious, dislodge the foreign object if it is visible and perform CPR. Severe cases of airway obstruction involve airway management until the obstruction can be removed at the hospital.

Another special condition is when the patient has a stoma, or an opening through the skin and into the trachea midway up the front of the neck. Stomas can either operate as independent airways or as a point of entry for a tracheostomy tube. One special consideration for a patient with a stoma is that the stoma must be humidified to prevent the formation of mucus plugs during ventilation. If patients with a stoma require oxygen, it should be delivered through a tracheostomy mask. If the patient has a tracheostomy tube and requires manual ventilation, the bag-mask can be attached directly to the tracheostomy tube. If the patient has only a stoma, then a child's mask can be attached to the bag. The mask is then placed directly over the stoma to ventilate.

Part 7: Respiratory Emergencies and Respiratory Conditions

Some emergencies will be directly related to the respiratory system. These include instances of damage or malfunction. In other instances, respiratory conditions will be secondary complications which must be factored in to the treatment plan. A brief description of some of the most common respiratory emergencies and conditions will now follow, along with how to identify them and recommendations for treatment. Remember that this should be used as a supplement and review for these conditions, and that each should be explored in greater depth.

One common condition encountered in the field is carbon dioxide retention. A range of lung diseases including COPD can result in chronically elevated levels of carbon dioxide in the patient's blood. In healthy individuals, increasing carbon dioxide levels trigger an increase in the rate and depth of inhalation. However, if the patient's body has adjusted to high levels of carbon dioxide, the body switches to hypoxic drive, meaning that low oxygen levels trigger an increase in the rate and depth of inhalation. If patients with a history of COPD require supplemental oxygen, it is important to use a low percentage of oxygen and take measures to ensure that as little carbon dioxide as possible is retained. Venturi masks are recommended in these instances, as they are designed with this purpose in mind.

Another common condition encountered in the field is dyspnea, an abnormal shortness of breath. Patients will exhibit rapid, shallow breath and anxiety. Dyspnea can occur for a variety of different reasons, including respiratory illnesses such as COPD or asthma. Other potential causes are anxiety, airway obstruction, and pulmonary edema. In order to effectively treat dyspnea, it is important to assess the patient to determine the underlying cause. Recommended treatment differs depending on the source. Hyperventilation is similar, in that it is an abnormal respiration rate. However, in the case of hyperventilation, the breathing is abnormally fast and often deeper than with dyspnea. It commonly results from fever, pain, or anxiety. As in the case of dyspnea, treatment for hyperventilation is aimed at addressing the underlying cause.

Another commonly encountered condition is asthma, a chronic respiratory condition which results in constriction and inflammation of the airways and increased production of mucus. Asthmatic patients will present with coughing, wheezing, and shortness of breath. Common treatment includes steroids and bronchodilators. Bronchodilators are medications which make breathing easier by relaxing the muscles in the lungs and widening the bronchi. Most asthma attacks are mild enough for home treatment. However, extremely acute asthma attacks, also known as status asthmaticus, may require emergency treatment or hospital care.

Hay fever is a respiratory condition which results from an allergic reaction. Symptoms of hay fever are excess mucus production and inflammation of the sinuses, alongside coughing, sneezing, and runny nose. Treatment involves decongestants and antihistamines. Another allergy-related respiratory condition is anaphylaxis. This is much more severe than hay fever and has the potential to be life-threatening. It may occur in response to a wide range of allergens, or substances which evoke allergic reactions, including nuts, shellfish, and bee stings.

Patients will exhibit trouble breathing, hives, and stridor. Blood pressure tends to drop with anaphylaxis, while the airways constrict. To treat anaphylactic patients, manage the airway and administer epinephrine.

Infections can occur in both the lower and upper airways. Potential causes of airway infection include pneumonia, croup, and Respiratory Syncytial Virus (RSV). One airway infection common in children and infants is bronchiolitis, an infection which causes inflammation and congestion in the bronchioles, the small airways in the lungs. Croup is a common respiratory virus in young children, and often presents with hoarseness, cough, and stridor. RSV is an extremely common respiratory virus with cold-like symptoms. RSV is mild in most cases, but can be more serious in infants and high-risk patients. Another, potentially more severe, infection of the upper respiratory tract is epiglottitis. This is an infection which causes swelling of the epiglottis and may block the airway. Epiglottitis is treated in the hospital with antibiotics; however, pre-hospital care includes airway management and potentially intubation. Patients with airway infections may present with dyspnea, cough, and wheezing, depending on the severity of the infection. Treatment is aimed at the underlying cause of the infection. Pre-hospital management includes oxygen, steroids, and bronchodilators.

Chronic obstructive pulmonary disease (COPD) is a blanket term for a number of diseases, including emphysema and chronic bronchitis, which cause progressive damage to the alveoli. COPD presents with the same symptoms as airway infections: dyspnea, coughing, and wheezing. Treatment for COPD is the same as the pre-hospital care for airway infections: oxygen, bronchodilators, and steroids.

If air or fluid collects outside of the lungs, it will constrict both the lungs and the blood vessels which perfuse them. If this is the result of air, the condition is termed spontaneous pneumothorax. The patient will exhibit symptoms of chest pain, shortness of breath, and decreased breath sounds in the affected area. Treatment involves the insertion of a chest tube into the pleural space to release air pressure.

Pleural effusion is a condition resulting from an accumulation of fluid in the pleural space. Symptoms are similar to those of spontaneous pneumothorax. Patients with pleural effusion will show symptoms of shortness of breath and decreased breath sounds in the affected area. However, the fluid must be removed in a hospital procedure. Therefore, pre-hospital management involves administering supplemental oxygen if the patient shows signs of hypoxia and keeping the patient as comfortable as possible while transporting them to the hospital.

Acute pulmonary edema is the accumulation of fluid within the lungs. One potential cause of the sudden onset of pulmonary edema is congestive heart failure. Patients will exhibit dyspnea, pink, frothy sputum, and cough. Crackles may also be heard in the lungs. Recommended treatment includes supplemental oxygen and furosemide. Furosemide is the generic name for Lasix.

Pulmonary embolism is another respiratory condition sometimes encountered in the field. Pulmonary embolism is a clot in a pulmonary artery. Often, the clot forms in another part of the body, most typically the legs, and then travels to the pulmonary artery. Once it has lodged in the pulmonary artery, it becomes potentially life-threatening. A pulmonary embolism restricts blood flow to the lungs and reduces oxygen levels in the blood and tissues. Patients will exhibit symptoms of dyspnea, hypoxia, and tachycardia, or abnormally rapid resting heart rate. Treatment involves the administration of blood thinners at the hospital. Pre-hospital treatment involves keeping the patient as comfortable as possible and providing supplemental oxygen is they show signs of hypoxia.

A number of extrinsic factors can interfere with the function of the respiratory system. These include environmental and industrial contaminants or the aspiration of a foreign body. Industrial and environmental contaminants involve the inhalation of gases, substances, or chemicals that irritate the airway or interfere with respiration. Carbon monoxide is one environmental contaminant which can interfere with respiration. It binds to the hemoglobin molecules and prevents the transfer of sufficient oxygen across the alveolar membrane. Patients exposed to environmental or industrial contaminants will exhibit signs of shortness of breath, altered levels of consciousness, and coughing. Treatment involves airway management and the administration of supplemental oxygen. If a foreign body is inhaled and obstructs the airway, patients will exhibit stridor and shortness of breath. Pre-hospital treatment involves supportive care and the management of the airway. The foreign body can then be removed once the patient has reached the hospital.

A number of complications can occur in patients with tracheostomy tubes. These include bleeding, dislodgement of the tube, and the blockage of the airway by mucus plugs. Any of these conditions can block the airway or result in poor oxygenation. Patients experiencing tracheostomy tube complications will exhibit symptoms of hypoxia and cyanosis. Proper treatment depends upon the underlying complication. Mucus plugs are one of the simplest to treat. In the event of a mucus plug in the tube, suction the tracheostomy tube and change the inner cannula.

Another condition encountered occasionally in the field is cystic fibrosis. Cystic fibrosis is a genetic condition, a chronic illness that affects the lungs and digestive system. Patients will present with shortness of breath, wheezing, and excessive production of mucus. Pre-hospital treatment involves oxygen, suctioning, and medication to loosen mucus.

Prior to the test, it's important to make sure that you are familiar with all procedures and the use of all equipment described above. Remember, this is not a comprehensive list. You will occasionally encounter other conditions which require special treatment. Some conditions will require the use of metered-dose inhalers or small-volume nebulizers. Metered-dose inhalers are small canisters used to deliver respiratory medication directly to the lungs. These inhalers are often used to administer bronchodilators or steroids. Bronchodilators are medications which open the airways, while steroids can be used to decrease inflammation. Small-volume nebulizers are also useful for delivering respiratory medications directly to the lungs. They generate a fine mist which can be used to carry a medication. This medication is then delivered to the lungs when the patient inhales the mist. Small-volume nebulizers are commonly used to administer the bronchodilator Albuterol to asthma patients and those with COPD.

Section 2: Cardiology and Resuscitation

The next most vital system to manage after respiration is the heart and circulatory system. An understanding of the circulatory system and its pathophysiology is vital to effective treatment of patients in emergency medical conditions. If the patient lacks a heartbeat, then resuscitation is the first priority. In order to understand possible cardiac and circulatory complications, it is necessary to fully comprehend the anatomy and physiology of the heart and circulatory system. This section explores cardiac anatomy and physiology, as well as the pathophysiology or potential disruptions that may be encountered during emergency medical services.

Next, this section explores CPR and resuscitation, including procedures and adjustments for patients with special conditions. This section also contains a review of chest pain and cardiac management, as well as complications with surgery patients and patients with cardiac assisting devices. A variety of cardiac terms are explored to help review your knowledge of the heart and its structure and function. Remember that this is used as a supplement and a review, rather than a replacement, of your course material. All special techniques discussed in this section should be reviewed more fully to ensure that you are fully familiar with their application.

Part 1: Cardiac Anatomy and Physiology

The center of the circulatory system is the heart. Arteries carry blood away from the heart. They divide into arterioles, which then divide further into capillaries. Capillaries suffuse the muscles, lungs, and tissues. They then rejoin into venules, extremely small veins that begin the journey of the blood back to the heart. Venules join together to form veins, which then carry blood back to the heart. The circulatory system carries oxygen and nutrients to all tissues, cells and organs within the body. The blood is also filtered by the kidneys so that waste products within the blood can be eliminated in the urinary tract. The blood also suffuses the intestines to absorb sugar and nutrients and deliver them to all cells and tissues. The flow of blood through the body is termed circulation.

The heart has four main chambers. These four chambers are the right and left ventricle and the right and left atrium. The atria are the upper chambers of the heart. They serve to collect a significant volume of blood and pump it into the ventricles. The ventricles then pump blood through the arteries. The left side of the heart deals with deoxygenated blood. The inferior and superior vena cava returns blood to the left atrium from the veins and capillaries that suffuse muscles and tissues. The left atrium then pumps blood into the left ventricle. The left ventricle pumps deoxygenated blood through the pulmonary artery, which divides to deliver this blood to both the right and left lung. The pulmonary artery quickly divides into arterioles, which then further divide into capillaries which suffuse the alveoli.

The capillaries which suffuse the alveoli then gather into venules and veins. Two pulmonary veins from each lung feed oxygenated blood into the left atrium of the heart. This blood is then pumped into the left ventricle. The wall of the left ventricle is significantly thicker than that of the right, as it is responsible for pumping blood all throughout the body. The left ventricle pumps oxygenated blood through the aorta, which divides into arteries that serve the brain, muscles, organs, and tissues. Two main coronary arteries split off of the aorta, feeding the heart oxygen-rich blood. The stroke volume is the volume of blood pumped through the left ventricle each beat, while the cardiac output is the stroke volume multiplied by the beats per minute, giving the total volume of blood pumped per minute.

The heart contains four main valves. Two of these valves are between the atria and ventricles. The tricuspid valve divides the right atrium and ventricle, preventing the blood pumped by the right ventricle from returning to the atrium. The bicuspid valve serves the same purpose for the left atrium and ventricle. The other two are termed semilunar valves and prevent blood from returning to the ventricles from the arteries. The aortic valve is situated between the left ventricle and aorta, while the pulmonary valve is situated between the right ventricle and the pulmonary artery.

The continued function of the heart is essential for survival. The heartbeat is the regular contraction of atria and ventricles. The continuity of contraction is governed by a function known as heart automaticity. Heart automaticity is maintained by the cardiac conduction system, a series of specialized bundles of cells in the myocardium, or muscular tissue of the heart, that generate a rhythm of electrical activity. These bundles of cells are the SA node, AV node, bundle of His, bundle branches, and Purkinje fibers.

The rate of the heartbeat is regulated by the autonomic nervous system. There are two functions of the autonomic nervous system which follow their own pathways. These are the sympathetic and parasympathetic nervous system. The sympathetic nervous system is responsible for shifting the body into "fight or flight" mode. When the sympathetic nervous system is activated, the blood vessels serving skeletal muscles and lungs dilate, or expand to permit additional blood flow, while those which serve the internal organs contract. Heart rate and blood pressure increase, alongside sweating and increased dilation of the pupils. Essentially, circulation is directed to the areas required for fast action, and away from the digestive system and other organs which facilitate long-term survival.

The parasympathetic nervous system essentially performs the opposite functions to those of the sympathetic nervous system. When the parasympathetic nervous system is activated, the heart rate slows, blood pressure reduces, the pupils contract, and blood vessels suffusing the internal organs and digestive system dilate. Through the process of dilation and contraction of selective portions of the circulatory system, blood is distributed efficiently to the areas that most need it. Optimal function of the circulatory system requires a sufficient volume of blood, selective dilation of the blood vessels, and healthy valves in both the heart and veins.

Part 2: Cardiac Pathophysiology
Heart disease is quite common. It is estimated that 25% of adults in the United States are affected by cardiac or circulatory conditions. One of the most common is atherosclerosis. This is a condition that affects the arteries. With atherosclerosis, the lumens, or inner tubular spaces of the arteries, begin to accumulate a fatty substance known as plaque.

Plaque is a combination of fat, cholesterol, and cellular waste products. As it builds up on the inner walls of the lumen, the walls thicken and lose elasticity. Hardened and thickened blood vessels are less able to dilate and contract to respond to different oxygen demands. The result is a reduction of blood flow, and, in some cases, a complete blockage. An ischemia is the term for an inadequate flow of blood to an organ or part of the body, often resulting from atherosclerosis.

When an artery is blocked completely, it is called an occlusion. Coronary occlusions are the cause of almost all heart attacks, known medically as myocardial infarctions. Acute myocardial infarctions are heart attacks resulting from a sudden loss of blood flow. In either cause, whether the myocardial infarction happens progressively or suddenly, the result is irreversible tissue damage to the affected region of the heart. This is not to be confused with a cardiac arrest, which is a sudden stop in heart function, though not directly related to atherosclerosis.

Total occlusions of an artery in the brain will result in a stroke. Plaque can also spill open into the blood vessel and cause blood clots to form. When these blood clots block blood flow to a major organ such as the heart or lungs, they are known as thromboembolisms. Clots can also lodge in the cerebral arteries and cause a stroke, form blockages in other major arteries, or enter a vein and cause deep vein thrombosis. Treatment for atherosclerosis usually involves lifestyle changes, medications such as angiotensin-converting enzyme (ACE) inhibitors, and Calcium blockers, and, in severe cases, surgery.

Myocardial ischemia, or an insufficient flow of blood to the heart muscles, can produce a collection of symptoms which produce conditions that into two categories, both of which are known as forms of acute coronary syndrome (ACS). The least harmful of these conditions is angina pectoris. Angina pectoris is caused by an arterial spasm or decreased flow of oxygen to the myocardium. Patients will experience pain and a sensation of squeezing or pressure in the mid-chest area. Other common symptoms are nausea and pain in the arm or jaw. In some instances, the symptoms may be mistaken for GERD, or gastroesophageal reflux disease. Angina pectoris, though painful, is not life threatening and does not cause tissue damage to the heart. However, it is a warning sign of heart disease. Patients experiencing angina pectoris should take preventative measures to reduce the risk of more serious conditions.

The second category of condition under the label of acute coronary syndrome is acute myocardial infarction. As described above, acute myocardial infarction can result from atherosclerosis and myocardial ischemia. It is a serious condition resulting from the sudden loss of arterial blood to the heart muscle, and causing irreversible tissue death to the affected area. Extreme cases can result in sudden death, and even less severe myocardial infarctions can cause lifelong death of regions of the heart. Symptoms are varied. In some instances, the patient experienced no symptomatic warnings of heart attack. However, typical symptoms include a squeezing or pressure sensation in the chest, sweating, nausea, and pain beginning in the chest and radiating to the abdomen, lower back, jaw, arm, or any combination of these areas. In some instances, the patient may syncope, or faint due to insufficient blood flow to the brain.

The likelihood of ACS is relatively low in younger individuals. Men tend to have a higher risk of suffering from acute coronary syndrome earlier in their lives. Risk factors include more than 45 years of age for men and more than 55 years of age for women. High cholesterol and blood pressure are significant risk factors, as is cigarette smoking and a lack of physical exercise. Obesity, unhealthy diet, and diabetes are also significant risk factors, as are family history of strokes, heart disease, or chest pain. In women, a family history of diabetes during pregnancy, preeclampsia, or high blood pressure is also a risk factor. Men are more likely to experience symptoms of chest pain, diaphoresis or sweating, and pain in the left arm. Women are more likely to experiencing myocardial infarction without chest pain, but with nausea.

A nitroglycerine regimen is a common form of management for acute coronary syndrome, as it can provide immediate widening of the coronary arteries and reduce the work of the heart. This can treat or prevent episodes of angina, but it is a form of symptom management rather than a curative measure. Aspirin and heparin are also common treatments for AMI. This is a condition with a high pre-hospital mortality rate.

In the event of acute myocardial infarction, the condition which actually causes damage is known as cardiogenic shock. Cardiogenic shock is clinically defined as decreased cardiac output which results in tissue hypoxia, eventually leading to organ damage or failure. In most cases, the time frame between acute myocardial infarction and cardiogenic shock is between five and six hours. Lower cardiac output can result in hypotension and insufficient oxygen to organs and tissues throughout the body. The patient will exhibit tachycardia, altered senses, cool extremities, and lowered urine output. Other symptoms include a weak pulse, a weak pulse, and pale skin. This is an extremely serious condition which requires hospital care. Emergency treatment involves supplemental oxygen, intravenous administration of fluids, and, if necessary, assisted ventilation.

Blood pressure is a measure of two factors: systolic and diastolic pressure. Systolic pressure is the pressure in the arteries resulting from the contraction of the heart. Diastolic pressure is the pressure in the arteries between heartbeats. Normal blood pressure for adults is considered 120/80 mmHg, or 120 mmHg systolic over 80 mmHg diastolic. Blood pressure is measured with an inflatable pressure cuff attached to a dial which reads the pressure in mmHg. The cuff is inflated enough to block blood flow, and then deflated slowly while the technician listens to the pulse through a stethoscope. The pressure is noted as it begins to flow through the cuffed area and again when full blood pressure is restored.

Blood pressure is considered high if it is above 140/90 mmHg. Hypertension, also known as chronic or acute high blood pressure, can become serious enough to require medical attention. Three conditions in particular are related to hypertensive conditions: aortic aneurysm, dissecting aortic aneurysm, and acute myocardial infarction. Aortic aneurysm is an enlargement of the aorta to up to 1.5 times the normal size. If the walls of the aorta have weakened, then excessively high or chronically high blood pressure can cause the aortic walls to bulge, and, in severe cases, to leak or rupture. Dissecting aortic aneurysms occur when the inner layer of the aorta tears and blood rushes through the tear, causing the middle and inner layers to separate or dissect.

Aortic aneurysms may not show symptoms until they enlarge or rupture. Large abdominal aortic aneurysms will tend to present with a throbbing, pulsing sensation near the navel, along with back pain and a deep, continuous pain in the abdomen or on the side of the abdomen. Large thoracic aortic aneurysms produce symptoms of back pain and pain or tenderness in the chest, as well as shortness of breath, hoarseness, and cough.

The rupture of an aortic aneurysm will result in sudden, intense tearing pain, centered either in the thoracic or abdominal region and radiating to the back or legs. Additional symptoms include dizziness, sweating, clamminess, profuse sweating, vomiting, and hypotension or low blood pressure. Secondary complications include the potential of blood clots to break away from the rupture and block blood flow in other parts of the circulatory system. If a dissecting aortic aneurysm ruptures, the patient will experience a sharp sudden pain in the back that radiates downwards, as well as pain in the arms, neck, jaw, or chest, as well as difficulty breathing. In the event that either an aortic or dissecting aortic aneurysm ruptures, the patient will suffer internal bleeding and must be gotten to the hospital as quickly as possible for emergency surgery.

Another cardiac emergency is congestive heart failure. In this condition, the cardiac output is insufficient to meet the body's needs. This can be caused by a number of conditions, but the result in all cases is slow blood flow throughout the body and the accumulation of fluid around the heart and in the lungs or tissues. Left heart failure occurs when the left ventricle cannot effectively pump blood throughout the body. Fluids will then back up into the lungs, causing pulmonary edema. Right heart failure occurs when the right ventricle cannot effectively pump blood through the lungs. Fluid will then build up in the tissues and organs, causing dependent edema. It is possible for both sides of the heart to fail, creating a condition known as biventricular heart failure. This is common, as left heart failure can often cause right heart failure.

Symptoms of congestive heart failure include rapid or irregular heartbeat, weakness and fatigue, and shortness of breath, especially in times of exertion, especially with right heart failure, as the blood is less able to reach the muscles and major organs. This may also result in dizziness and confusion, as less blood can effectively reach the brain. Fluid and water retention is a sign of right heart failure. This may also cause an increased output of urine at night and a loss of appetite. With left heart failure, the lungs will become congested and the shortness of breath will become more extreme, especially when at rest or lying in bed. This is often accompanied by a dry hack or cough, a cracking sound in the lungs, or wheezing. Patient should be assessed for hypoxia and provided supplemental oxygen. As soon as patient contact is made 100% oxygen should be administered via non-rebreather mask. This will help maximize oxygen concentration and saturate hemoglobin. Treatments may also include the CPAP device (continuous positive airway pressure) CPAP is probably the biggest change in CHF treatment in the past few decades. It often will decrease the need for endotracheal intubations. Consult local protocols. Common treatment also involves the use of diuretics such as furosemide (Lasix). Patient should be made as comfortable as possible en route to the hospital.

Part 3: Patient Assessment in Event of a Cardiac Emergency

Effective treatment of cardiac emergencies requires a quick and accurate assessment of the situation, including the environment, current conditions of the patient, medical history, and medication regimens. Timely assessment is critical for the best patient outcome. The first step in assessment (in any type of emergency) is to size up the scene. Information gathering should begin with the 911 call. The five basic components of the scene size-up include the number of patients involved in the emergency, the nature of the illness or mechanism of injury, resource determination, standard precautions including BSI or Body-Safety-Isolation, and scene safety.

In typical situations, cardiac emergencies involve a single patient. Make sure that all cardiac-related resources are at hand prior to arriving on the scene, including oxygen and an automated external defibrillator (AED). If possible, ensure that advanced life support (ALS) backup is on the way. BSI and scene safety concerns are minimal, but universal precautions should be taken. One you arrive on the scene, it is important to observe the environment and obtain all possible information about the incident from the witnesses and, if possible, the patient. If necessary, make sure that the environment is stable. While assessing the scene, find out about the onset of the incident and the environment surrounding the incident, as well as the duration and pattern of symptoms and signs. Keep an open mind to avoid jumping to conclusions regarding the nature of the emergency.

After sizing up the scene, move on to primary assessment. This should be done within moments after arrival. Primary assessment involves checking the patient for any life-threatening injuries or conditions. A useful mnemonic to keep in mind is ABC: airway, breathing, and circulation. Open and maintain the airway without obstruction, then make sure the patient is breathing. Next, check the patient's pulse. If the patient is not breathing or lacks a pulse, unless otherwise indicated, perform CPR . Also assess whether or not the patient is alert and, if so, their level of consciousness.

Once it has been confirmed that the patient is stable, take the patient's history. Some patient history may have been obtained during the scene assessment, but ensure that all other relevant details have been obtained. Remain calm and use common terms instead of medical terminology. Speaking clearly and concisely, find out the medication regimen, contraindicated medications, and medical history from the witnesses and patient. Gather all possible information about symptoms and signs, as well as a history of any related or similar incidents and comorbid conditions.

There are a number of key questions which may be asked to the alert patient. Ask about dyspnea or trouble breathing. A common symptom of heart failure is orthopnea, or increased work of breathing when lying down. To assess orthopnea, a patient can be asked how many pillows they use to prop themselves up when they sleep. The patient can be asked about palpitations. These are experienced as a pounding in the chest or a sensation of skipped or rapid heartbeats. Frequency, duration, and precipitating factors can help to identify the source of the cardiac emergency. Also ask about syncope, or incidents of dizziness, vertigo, lightheadedness, or loss of consciousness presenting alongside weakness. Abnormalities in heart rate or blood pressure are potential causes of syncope.

Another key question regards fatigue. The oxygen deficit that leads to heart failure is often exhibited in patients prior to angina or myocardial infarction. Fatigue is also a common symptom of anemia, so it must be taken into consideration alongside other symptoms. It is important to ask the patient about coughing, as this can be a sign of pulmonary edema, pulmonary infarction, pulmonary hypertension, thoracic aortic aneurysm, and a number of other cardiac conditions. If the coughing is accompanied by bloody sputum, it can be an indication of pulmonary edema, pulmonary embolism, or pulmonary infarction.

While asking these questions, also look for signs of edema, cyanosis, or skin irregularities around the client's eyes or within the eye around the iris. Edema is a sign of elevated venous pressure and possible heart failure. Cyanosis is a sign of hypoxia and a signal that the patient requires supplemental oxygen. Raised, yellowing areas of tissue around the eyes are a symptom of high cholesterol. Light grey rings around the iris also indicate high cholesterol levels and often accompany heart disease. Examining the patient for symptoms such as this is the beginning of the secondary assessment, an evaluation of the patient aimed at identifying the specific cardiac condition.

When questioning the patient, remember the OPQRST mnemonic for pain assessment. This mnemonic stands for Onset, Provocation or Palliation, Quantity and Quality, Region and Radiation, Severity, and Timing. Onset refers to when the pain began. The patient can be asked what triggers or causes the pain to determine provocation, and what improves or lessons the pain to determine palliation. Regarding quality, the pain may be described as tearing, stabbing, throbbing, burning, crushing, stretching, or any number of other qualitative descriptors. Each gives clues as to the underlying cause of the emergency. For region and radiation, ask the patient where it hurts, whether the pain has moved to continues to move through the body, how far the pain extends, etc. Severity of pain can be assessed on a scale of one to ten. 1 being mild pain and 10 being extremely severe pain. Finally, timing can both assess the current incident and any history of similar incidents, as well as when during the day, season, or schedule the pain arises.

Other aspects of the secondary assessment include examining all aspects of the patient to identify the specifics of the condition. Take note of the current symptoms of the dysfunction. Assess the condition of cardiovascular, circulatory, and respiratory systems. Observe the obvious physical indicators, such as quality of breathing and skin coloration. Note body temperature and temperature of the extremities. Check capillary refill by pressing firmly on the sternum for five seconds, and noting how quickly color returns to the area after pressure is released. Check turgor by pinching and lifting a bit of skin from the back of the hand or collarbone and observing how quickly it returns to position. Monitor pulse, blood pressure, and oxygen saturation. Auscultate lungs and heart, using a stethoscope to listen to the four main areas where the heart sounds are loudest, and to both lungs, from the back and front if possible. You may wish to review the procedure for assessing lungs and heart.

When making your assessment, it is important to remember that signs and symptoms of cardiac emergency can be confused with respiratory dysfunctions or indigestion. One of the most common signs of cardiac emergency is chest pain. The quality of this pain may be squeezing, pressure, or fullness. Pain may radiate to other parts of the body, including the jaw and teeth, stomach, neck, back, and one or both arms. Pain may be brought about by activity, and may come and go. This is common in cases of heart attack. Trouble breathing is another common sign, especially if the difficulty worsens when the patient is in a lying position. Palpitations are also common as well, and persistent palpitations should be evaluated in the event that they indicate life-threatening arrhythmias. Coughing is another common symptom, and is often an indicator of pulmonary edema or pulmonary hypertension. Bloody sputum is also possible in the case of pulmonary edema and a key sign of heart failure.

Other possible symptoms of cardiac emergency include syncope, such as dizziness, vertigo, or sudden lack of consciousness along with a period of weakness. Patients may exhibit sweating, nausea, vomiting, anxiety, a sudden onset of severe pain, and unexplained fatigue. If any of the above symptoms are observed in a patient, watch out for cyanosis, high or low blood pressure, elevated or low heart rates, edema, or engorged or pulsating veins. Also look out for abnormal breathing. Finally, if the patient is unable to breathe normally when the head is tilted up, then this is a strong indicator of heart failure. Chest pain is the most common symptom for both men and women. Women are more likely than men to exhibit symptoms like fatigue, nausea, vomiting, or pain in the abdomen, shoulder, neck, and upper back.

While some of these symptoms may be confused with respiratory distress, as a whole, they will allow you to determine that the emergency is cardiac in origin. Respiratory emergency symptoms, on the other hand, include shallow or labored breathing, breathing sounds or sounds in the lungs including wheezing, stridor, crackling or gurgling, and coughs. Other symptoms include confusion and anxiety, tracheal tugging, see-sawing of the chest and abdomen, nasal flaring, the retraction of the intercostal muscles or use of the neck muscles when breathing, or head bobbing in the attempt to breathe. Patients may exhibit pursed lips and difficulty talking. The patient may sweat in the effort to breathe and the pulse will be abnormal. Patients will also tend to become hypoxic and show cyanosis as they become deprived of oxygen. Indigestion, on the other hand, can have symptoms of chest pain similar to heart attack. However, if this is the case, then this pain will most likely be accompanied by sweating, shortness of breath, or any of the other symptoms listed above.

After the secondary assessment, the patient should be prepared for transport to the hospital. Administer any additional treatment required by the patient. At this point, it is necessary to do a reassessment of the patient's condition. In essence, the reassessment evaluates vital signs in the same way as the primary assessment while preparing to communicate the patient's condition to the ER team. Keep an eye on the patient's current status, as well as any changes to this status. Reassess the primary concern or complaint. If necessary, adjust treatment to facilitate improvement or address any worsening of the patient's condition. Remember to reassess vital signs every five minutes for unstable patients, and every fifteen for stable patients.

Part 4: Chest Pain or Discomfort, Cardiac Monitoring, and Age Concerns

Though chest pain is the most indicative sign of cardiac emergency, it can be a result of a number of other causes as well. Given the potential severity of cardiac emergencies, and the need to respond quickly in order to save the life of a patient suffering from a cardiac emergency, it is important to assess the patient accurately and provide treatment if necessary. Basic treatment ranges from making the patient comfortable in the mildest cases, to administering oxygen and medication and transporting the patient to the hospital in the most severe cases. Be sure to know the signs of different cardiac emergencies, so that the pre-hospital treatment can be tailored to the patient's needs.

In mild cases of chest pain, it may be unnecessary to do more than attend to basic measures for comfort. Position the client to relieve as much pain or discomfort as possible. If their clothing is confining or uncomfortable, adjust or remove it as necessary. Low doses of acetylsalicylic acid, also known as ASA or aspirin, may be helpful for improving patient outcomes. Aspirin can help prevent blood clots from forming as a preventative measure for heart attacks and strokes. The patient may be administered one dose of 325 mg aspirin by the EMT if presenting with symptoms of ACS. However, no aspirin should be administered if the patient is allergic to aspirin, if the patient has taken 325mg of aspirin one hour or less from the time of treatment, if their blood pressure is over 180/110 mmHg, or if there is the patient is suspected of having gastrointestinal bleeding.

If the patient requires supplemental oxygen, first determine the appropriate equipment for oxygen delivery. Administer oxygen at as low a flow as possible to achieve the best patient outcome. In this scenario 100% oxygen via a non rebreather mask in typically recommended. While monitoring the blood oxygen levels with pulse oximetry, dial the flow rate of supplemental oxygen slowly, ensuring that the blood oxygen levels do not fall below 92%.

Nitroglycerin is another medication often used to treat cardiac emergency. If the patient is experiencing symptoms of angina pectoris, acute myocardial infarction, or pulmonary edema with hypertension, they meet the criteria for administration. If the patient has had previous incidents of cardiovascular episodes, then they will most likely have a prescription for nitroglycerin. Patients with a prescription for nitroglycerin with these symptoms should receive it without delay. Nitroglycerin dosage should be 0.4g administered sublingually in tablet or spray form. If symptoms persist, administer a second dose in five minutes. One more dose may be administered after another five minutes. The maximum dosage for EMT administration is three doses at intervals of five minutes.

Patients should absolutely not be administered nitroglycerin for the following reasons: known sensitivity to nitrate medications, conditions of hypotension, severe anemia, or intracranial pressure. Also avoid the use of nitroglycerin if the patient is below twelve years of age or if they have taken any medication for erectile dysfunction in the last twenty four hours. Be cautious about the use of nitroglycerin with patients that exhibit an elevated or low heart rate, with patients that are intoxicated or under the effects of alcohol, and with those on medication for high blood pressure.

Nitroglycerin is inactivated by light, heat, and moisture, so tablets should be kept in amber glass containers with tight-fitting lids. Remember to remove the cotton from the bottle. Patients should not chew or swallow nitroglycerin tablets, but should place them under the tongue and allow them to absorb. Sprays should not be shaken and should be stored away from heat and direct light. When administering the spray, ensure that no providers inhale the medication due to proximity or a poorly-aimed spray. Gloves should be worn when handling nitroglycerin patches or paste to prevent the medication from absorbing due to contact with the skin. Nitroglycerin has a shelf life of three months after opening, and it should never be consumed after the expiration date on the bottle. Nitroglycerin should also be handled with care to avoid cross-contamination between patients.

During transport, the patient's heart should be monitored with an ECG machine. Depending on your jurisdiction, you may be working with a four lead or twelve lead ECG, so it's important to know the proper electrode placement for the type you'll be using in the field. If the placement of an electrode is off by as little as two inches, it can cause artifacts in the ECG readout. Artifacts are inaccurate readings. They can potentially conceal abnormal heart activity or indicate heart conditions where none exist.

In order to get an accurate ECG reading, the skin must be prepared before placing the electrodes. Obvious chest hair should be shaved prior to placement. If the patient is sweating, then the perspiration should be wiped clean with clean gauze or a towel. Remove skin oil with an alcohol pad, and scrub firmly to remove the outer layer of epidermis. After the skin is prepared, connect the monitoring cables to the electrodes. Apply the electrode to the proper position, and then press the center firmly down to ensure maximum contact with the skin. Placement of many of the electrodes should be below the left breast of female patients, and in line vertically with the proper anatomical placement in obese patients.

In children, chest pain is often benign. It is experienced most frequently as a response to acute illness, and tends to be self-limiting, or resolved without need for treatment. If a child has no congenital heart defect or previous history of cardiac events, then the most likely cause of a cardiac event is a respiratory issue. Choking is one such respiratory issue which can precipitate a minor cardiac event, and in most cases this event becomes resolved as the respiratory event is resolved. A congenital heart defect or CHD is a defect present at birth, and this condition should be easily obtainable from the patient's medical history. Emergency responders should treat even minor cardiac events as serious in CHD patients. Pre-hospital treatment mostly consists of supportive care, along with high-flow oxygen and possible endotracheal intubation if the patient experiences severe dyspnea.

There are a number of complications common with older patients experiencing a cardiac emergency. It is of utmost importance to obtain a medical history and to provide timely treatment. Geriatric patients may have vague or absent symptoms, and they may tend to delay seeking treatment. The number of pacemaker cells in the sinus node of the heart tends to decrease with age, so there is a higher likelihood of cardiac arrest or asystole. Heart rhythm tends to be less regular, and geriatric patients also have a higher risk of tachycardia. Cardiac output is also diminished, meaning that any damage to the heart is less easily tolerated and conditions resulting from insufficient cardiac output are more prevalent. Geriatric patients tend to have higher mortality, so it is extremely important to perform an accurate and quick assessment and administer treatment without delay. It is also possible for geriatric patients to have altered levels of consciousness prior to an emergency event, so it may be more difficult to obtain information during the assessment process.

Part 5: Cardiac Assistive Devices and Defibrillators

Heart rate is naturally regulated by several pacemaker nodes, or bundles of cells that produce rhythmic electrical activity which then triggers contractions of the myocardium. These nodes are the heart's natural pacemakers. They coordinate the contraction of different parts of the heart by creating an electrical conduction pathway which triggers atria and ventricles in turn. The first bundle is the sinoatrial or SA node. The electrical signal from the SA node begins the contraction of the atria. The electrical signal then travels to the AV or atrioventricular node, which transfers the signal to the ventricles. Next, the charge travels to the Bundle of His where the charge is divided along the right and left bundle branches to the right and left ventricles. The bundle branches lead to thin electrical fibers which cause the ventricles to contract. This electrical pathway causes the ventricles to contract directly after the atria have contracted, ensuring that the pattern of contractions have the optimal effect on blood flow

There are two surgically implanted devices often encountered in the field which support the electrical conduction system of the heart or provide electrical stimulation. It is critical for the EMT to know about these devices and understand how to adjust treatment when they are present. Many patients with pre existing heart conditions will be fitted with pacemakers, which artificially stimulate the pacemaker nodes of the heart to maintain regular heart rhythm. Another common device is the ICD or Implantable Cardiac Defibrillator. This device is surgically placed in the abdominal area or chest. It monitors the heart rate and delivers a shock to the heart when it exhibits potentially life-threatening arrhythmia. This includes bradycardia, an abnormally slow heart rate, or tachycardia, and abnormally fast heart rate. The shock delivered by an ICD simulates the heart's natural electrical conduction pathway. ICD patients with a cardiac emergency should be supplemented with titrated oxygen and monitored with a 12-lead ECG. Contact the receiving hospital as soon as possible and request an ALS/ILS intercept.

Chest compressions can be performed on ICD patients and patients with pacemakers. If an ICD device delivers a shock during compressions, providers without gloves will feel a slight tingling sensation, but will not receive damage. An AED or automated external defibrillator can be used on these patients as well, though this can damage the device. Remember to set the AED on the lowest setting. If working with a patient with an ICD, wait until the ICD cycle has finished prior to defibrillation. Place the pads in clinically accepted positions as far as possible from the device. Try to place them a minimum of one inch away from the device placement. Providers may also wish to use the posterior or anterior pad positions. If a patient with an ICD or pacemaker is defibrillated, the device should be examined after emergency treatment to make sure that it still works properly.

Another device commonly encountered in patients with pre existing heart conditions is the defibrillator vest. This device monitors a patient's cardiac activity and delivers a high-energy shock similar to an AED when detecting a treatable arrhythmia. Prior to this shock, the vest will issue vibrations and an audible warning. Responders should make sure not to touch the vest when the shock is delivered, as they may be shocked as well. Shocks will last from 25 to 60 seconds, depending on the rate and type of the arrhythmia.

Compressions can be issued through the vest if necessary. If the vest is interfering with chest compressions, the battery can be removed from the device and the device can be removed. If it is necessary to use an AED, the device should be removed prior to defibrillation. The responder may see a blue gel on the patient's skin. This is secreted by the device to facilitate defibrillation and mitigate burns. It can be removed with water prior to use of the AED. The device and battery should be brought to the hospital along with the battery. This will allow the patient to download event data and recharge the battery.

The responder may encounter patients wearing a Left Ventricular Assist Device or LVAD. The LVAD is a surgically implanted device that supports the action of the left ventricle. LVADs are used to support heart function in patients requiring a heart transplant. It acts as a bridging life support mechanism prior to the availability of a donor heart. The LVAD can be set to pulsatile flow, mimicking the natural action of the heart, or continuous flow. Pulsatile LVADs are being phased out due to the recent innovation of the continuous setting. Providers should remember that patients with LVAD devices cannot be palpated to determine blood pressure.

Auscultate the patient for a precordial or epigastric hum, which indicates the failure of the device. Obtain blood pressure with a manual pressure cuff inflated past 120 mmHg, and then listen for the brachial pulse with a Doppler while slowly deflating the cuff. Check the external controller device, noting the pump speed, flow, power, and battery life of the external controller. Then, monitor heart function with an ECG. Make sure to familiarize yourself with the optimal functioning range of the LVAD and troubleshooting procedures.

Part 6: AED or Automated External Defibrillator

The AED is a device used in the field to resuscitate a patient by providing an electric shock to the body to reset the electrical conduction system of the heart. AEDs are computerized, interactive, and semi-automated. They have been designed to be as simple as possible, so that they can be used by non-medical personnel in the event of an emergency. AEDs have become a widespread companion to the emergency responder and have dramatically increased survival rate for patients with cardiac emergencies. The AED both monitors the activity of the heart in the same manner as an ECG and delivers a pulse of electricity when life-threatening arrhythmias are detected. Two dangerous arrhythmias which will trigger the electric pulse of the AED are ventricular fibrillation and ventricular tachycardia. Ventricular fibrillation is a condition in which the ventricles are quivering in an unorganized fashion, while ventricular tachycardia is when the ventricles contract so quickly that they cannot effectively pump blood. Ventricular tachycardia will often lead to ventricular fibrillation.

It is important for responders to understand the five links to the chain of survival in the event of cardiac emergency. These links are: 1. Recognition of cardiac arrest and activation of the emergency response system. 2. Early CPR, emphasizing chest compressions. 3. Rapid defibrillation. 4. Basic and advanced emergency care services. And, 5. Advanced life support and post-cardiac arrest care.

Responders should use a defibrillator on patients without a palpable pulse that show signs of cardiac emergency. The defibrillator will monitor the patient's heart activity and provide a shock when necessary. Be sure to be familiar with the function and precautions regarding defibrillators and follow instructions prior to delivering a shock. The main reasons to avoid the use of a defibrillator are if it cannot obtain an accurate analysis of the patient's cardiac activity or if it might pose a hazard to the responders or others around the patient. Avoid using the defibrillator in wet conditions, as this may result in electric shock to the responder or bystanders. Also make sure to dry the patient fully prior to defibrillation. If transdermal patches are found on the patients, remove the patches with a gloved hand and wipe all residue and gel free of the skin prior to defibrillation. Make sure you are familiar with alternative AED pad placements so that defibrillation can be administered without delay.

Make sure that the AED electrodes are placed correctly and in full contact with the skin, otherwise artifacts could lead to unnecessary shocks or miss life-threatening arrhythmias. Body hair may interfere with the adhesion of AED electrodes, thus skewing the readings. Other conditions like the vibration and motion of a moving vehicle can also interfere with AED accuracy. In most conditions, however, defibrillators are safe to use and recommended for resuscitation of patients experiencing nearly any cardiac emergency. The advantages of a defibrillator are vast, especially in the instance of sudden cardiac arrest. AEDs can be operated effectively by an individual without training. They can monitor heart activity and issue shocks when necessary. With the use of an AED, survival rates for SCA victims rise from 2.5% to nearly 80%.

CPR education is widespread and has improved patient outcomes in cardiac emergencies significantly. One implication of this widespread education is that responders will often arrive on scene where CPR is already being administered on the patient. If the patient has been effectively resuscitated with CPR, then the responder should monitor, assess, and take all further measures as necessary. If the patient is still in asystole, meaning that they lack discernible heart activity, then the responder should administer shock with the AED as soon as possible.

The defibrillator must be properly maintained in order to be effective in the field. Part of the scope of work for emergency responders is regular preventative maintenance (PM) and quality checks of all equipment. These are important for all equipment and materials, and absolutely critical to ensure that the AED is functioning properly when the responder arrives on the scene. Each jurisdiction has requirements for PM and quality checks, so make sure to be familiar for the procedures required by your jurisdiction. Also make sure to familiarize yourself with the operating handbook for your make and model of AED so that preventative maintenance addresses all necessary areas. Finally, make sure that all emergency personnel are fully trained and familiarized with the proper function and maintenance of all emergency medical equipment.

Preventative maintenance for an AED begins with regularly checking the status indicator of the machine. The machine will self-monitor daily and give indications of malfunctioning circuitry. If malfunctions are detected, the machine will give these results in the readout and, in some cases, with a series of audible chirps. The AED must also be examined daily for obvious exterior damage. Batteries should be replaced every four years, and pads should be replaced every two years. Check the operating manual to see if replacement needs are different for your model, and always follow manufacturer replacement guidelines.

Conduct monthly inspections and keep a log. Note damage or missing parts, check the battery, pads, and cables and replace as needed. These same checks should be done before using the AED in the field. Also prior to use in the field, download data from internal memory to a computer or memory storage unit. After ensuring that the equipment itself is undamaged, the most important aspect of maintenance is to ensure that the battery is fully charged prior to arrival on the scene. 45% of device problems leading to fatalities are associated with insufficiently charged batteries.

If any manufacturer malfunction is observed in the AED device, it should be reported immediately, and the device should be exchanged with one that functions properly. This is critical for saving lives in the field. In addition, improper use of an AED in the field or use of an improperly maintained AED can have legal ramifications. Medical supervision is important to ensure that guidelines, procedures, and protocols are being followed in AED use. This falls under the purview of the medical director. The responders should be debriefed by the medical director after each use of the AED, if possible, to facilitate quality improvement of AED procedures.

Both AEDs and manual defibrillators can be used on children. Manual defibrillators work just like AEDs, but they should only be used by trained professionals. When working with children, it may be necessary to adjust the type of device and type of pad. Smaller paddles should be used for children than adults, and care should be taken to ensure that the pads don't overlap. With this in mind, the largest paddle possible should be used. Pediatric dose attenuators should be used for all defibrillation on children below eight years of age, if possible. The pediatric dose attenuator adjusts the level of electric shock to 50 J to make sure that the electric "dose" is suitable for children. If no pediatric dose attenuator is available, set the machine on the lowest settings.

Part 7: Cardiac Arrest Care

Cardiac arrest is one of the more common cardiac emergencies, and it is important for the emergency responder to be prepared to encounter it in the field. Remember that cardiac arrest is not the same as a heart attack. Heart attack is a condition in which blood flow to a portion of the heart is blocked. In cardiac arrest, the contraction of the heart ceases. Sudden cardiac arrest or SCA is life-threatening. Patient mortality rates are high if the patient is not resuscitated within a few minutes. As with all cardiac emergencies, a timely response is critical to ensure best patient outcomes. In order to facilitate a prompt response, members of the emergency response team should be assigned roles. Scene assessment, primary assessment, CPR or defibrillation, assessment of MOI or mechanism of injury, all aspects of the immediate response should be assigned so that the team can coordinate their response as quickly and efficiently as possible.

Begin CPR immediately, and coordinate defibrillation with compressions. Rotate team members to avoid exhaustion. If the patient is unresponsive, then the AED should be used as soon as possible. Pause compressions when administering shock, and then continue CPR, beginning with compressions, after the shock has been administered. The AED will direct the process after it has been put into play. Alternate between AED shocks and compressions until ROSC, or the return of spontaneous circulation. In other words, continue until the patient's heartbeat resumes. The return of spontaneous circulation is an indication that the patient has regained adequate blood flow after a cardiac arrest. After ROSC, monitor the patient to ensure that they are stable until they can be transferred to emergency room personnel. Always follow current guidelines for resuscitation .

There are three possibilities after defibrillation. The patient will either regain a pulse, the patient will not regain a pulse and the AED will recommend shock, or the patient will have no pulse and the machine will not recommend shock. If the patient has regained a pulse, monitor them and administer any other necessary medical procedures to ensure that they are stabilized. If the AED recommends shock, continue to alternate defibrillation and CPR. In the case that there is no pulse and the machine does not recommend defibrillation, refer to the guidelines of your jurisdiction for proper handling of the situation.

It is critical to monitor the patient during transport. The patient may experience cardiac arrest or become unconscious during transport. If this is the case, then it is necessary to resuscitate the patient. Administer resuscitation according to ALS guidelines and the best practice recommendations in your jurisdiction. When working with ALS personnel, make sure to communicate clearly and concisely. However, if ALS is not yet on the scene and the patient enters ventricular fibrillation, use the AED promptly. Make sure to familiarize yourself with the scope of practice both of EMT and ALS to understand the appropriate guidelines and roles for emergency medical service.

The role of BLS, or Basic Life Support, in resuscitation is to recognize a life-threatening situation and provide high quality care for patients requiring CPR or experiencing cardiac or other medical emergencies. The function of BLS is to sustain life in the event of cardiac arrest, airway emergencies, or respiratory conditions. For basic life support, the ABC mnemonic is central: airway, breathing and circulation. Make sure that the airway is free of obstruction, ensure that the patient is breathing, and make sure that they either have a heartbeat or immediately receive compressions or defibrillation. If the patient is not breathing begin ventilations with a bag valve mask right away. Current medical advice suggests that patient outcome is better when chest compressions are addressed first, changing the acronym to CAB: chest compressions, airway, and breathing. For basic life support, the EMT should ensure that the patient is breathing, their airway is open, that they have a pulse, and that there is no bleeding. ALS, or advanced life support, extends beyond BLS in that it provides more intensive monitoring and the administration of medications and IV fluids.

Part 8: CPR (Cardiopulmonary Resuscitation)

CPR is one of the most important techniques that the emergency responder can learn. If the patient is unresponsive and lacks a pulse, it is important to begin CPR immediately, starting with chest compressions. Ideal rate for compressions is 100 per minute. Avoid leaning on the chest between compressions to allow the chest to recoil as much as possible between compressions. The purpose of CPR is ROSC, the return of spontaneous circulation and breathing. The five critical steps of CPR are: begin compressions, check the airway, give two breaths, resume compressions as long as necessary, communicate and collaborate with ALS and ER teams. The chain of survival in situations requiring CPR is: recognition of cardiac emergency and contacting emergency responders, CPR, emphasizing chest compressions, rapid defibrillation, basic life support and emergency medical services, and advanced life support with post-cardiac arrest care.

Remember that CPR should not be initiated on patients that have a palpable pulse, even if they are unresponsive. Also, if the patient has an open airway and adequate respiration, then it is not necessary to provide artificial ventilations. So, check for pulse and airway before beginning compressions. CPR should not be done if patients have a pulse but are not breathing, though respiratory support should be provided. Other conditions which negate the need for CPR include do not resuscitate orders or DNRs, patients with rigor mortis or liver mortis, and patients with no signs of life. Always check with your medical director if in doubt.

Eventually, it will be time to stop CPR. The goal is to continue until the patient no longer needs it or until better care is available. The mnemonic STOP can be helpful for the responder in knowing the appropriate time to cease CPR resuscitation. STOP means: starts breathing, transfer of care, out of strength, physician's order. When the patient begins breathing and once more has a pulse, CPR has done its job in the best possible way. If more capable care arrives before this point, transfer the patient into the hands of ALS, paramedic, or ER personnel. If the responder is out of strength, they are no longer helpful to the patient and risk injury to themselves. And, if the physician orders the CPR to stop, it means that it is no longer required.

When transferring care, it may be necessary to interrupt CPR. Try to minimize the interruptions as much as possible. Potential interruptions include lifting the patient for transport. The chest compression fraction is defined as the amount of time that chest compressions are administered after cardiac cessation out of the total time that the heart is not functioning. The higher the chest compression fraction, the higher the survival rate. It's important to remember that CPR is not enough. Consider scene safety, the cause of the event itself, and information gathering from witnesses and bystanders. Information from these sources will help to frame the most effective emergency treatment plan.

The patient will be most amenable to assessment and CPR when they are placed in a supine position on a firm, flat surface. Supine is when the patient is lying down on their back and facing up, as opposed to the prone position where they are lying on their front facing down. Try to make sure that you have enough space for at least two responders and all necessary equipment. If patients are spontaneously breathing and have no spinal injury, then they should be log rolled into the recovery position. Before beginning compressions, take ten seconds to try to arouse the patient and check for pulse and breathing. To palpate the carotid artery for a pulse, place the fingers near the upper neck between the sternomastoid and trachea at about the level of the cricoid cartilage. Check for breathing by looking or the rise and fall of the chest and by bending low to listen for sounds of breath or feel for breath with the cheek.

If the patient has no pulse, begin chest compressions. Kneel next to the patient, place one hand on top of the other in the standard position. Place two fingers at the sternum where the lower ribs meet. Place the heel of the other hand just next to the fingers closer to the head. Place the other hand on top of the first with the fingers laced together and give compressions at a depth of two inches, at a rate of 100 per minute. Provide one breath every 5-6 seconds via bag valve mask, provided you have two rescuers. Do not cease chest compressions when providing breaths. Each breath should last one second, and the chest should visibly rise. Make sure that the arms are extended and the responder performing CPR is vertically aligned above the patient. This will help to avoid exhaustion and injury to the responder. The rescuers should rotate between compressions and ventilations every 5 cycles of CPR to avoid fatigue. Depending on local protocols, you may as an EMT be able to insert an advanced airway such as a King airway.

When dealing with infants and children, you'll need to make adjustments in hand placement and breaths. The rate of chest compressions for both infants and children is the same as that for adults: 100 per minute. When dealing with infants and children less than one year old, reduce the depth of compressions to 1.5 inches. When a single responder is available for CPR, they should kneel by the side of the patient and use two fingers to compress the chest just below the line of the nipples. Two breaths should be given for each thirty compressions for single rescuer CPR. If two responders are administering CPR, one should kneel at the feet of the patients and give compressions with two hands encircling the chest. The other responder should kneel at the head and provide one breath for every fifteen compressions or if using a bag valve mask they should ventilate the child once every 3 seconds making sure the chest clearly rises.

With children from one year old to puberty, place either one or two hands on the lower half of the breastbone. Just as with infants, the ratio of compressions to breaths will depend on the number of responders administering CPR. Depth of compressions is two inches, just as with adults. A single responder should give two breaths for each 30 compressions. For two responders, two breaths should be given for each fifteen compressions or once every 3 seconds using a bag valve mask. Remember that cardiac arrest is uncommon in pediatric patients without a history of cardiac events, congenital heart defects, or respiratory conditions that lead to cardiac complications.

Part 9: Airway Obstructions

One of the most important early response techniques is to check the airway to see that it is open and unobstructed, and maintain it during resuscitation. The airway may be blocked by food, aspirated objects, or even the tongue. Prior to providing breaths in CPR, it is important to open the airway. The techniques are simple, and have been described in the section on respiration. To provide a brief review: use the head tilt-chin lift if patients are not suspected of having a spinal injury. Use the jaw-thrust as an alternative to reduce risk of spinal injury. The jaw-thrust is contraindicated if the patient has severe facial damage. However, spinal injury takes priority over facial injury if both are present. Even in the case of possible spinal injury, opening the airway takes precedence, as this will immediately save the patient's life.

Prior to beginning resuscitation, open the airway following the proper maneuver and check for obstructions. One of the most common obstructions is the tongue. The techniques for opening the airway are designed to pull the tongue away from the pharynx. However, it is possible that the patient has some extrinsic obstruction. Signs may include choking or gagging sounds, coughing, stridor, high-pitched gasping, wheezing, agitation, and confusion. The patient may also be completely unable to make a sound if their airway is blocked completely. The reflexive gesture for choking involves hands placed around the throat. Finally, if patients have been unable to breathe long enough to become hypoxic, then their skin and lips will begin to turn blue and they will become unconscious.

In the event of airway obstruction, main techniques include the abdominal thrust and chest thrust. The abdominal thrust is the preferred technique. This is also known as the Heimlich maneuver. This is performed by standing behind the patient and wrapping both arms around them. Make a fist with one hand and place it below the sternum and above the navel. Grasp the fist with the other hand and administer sharp upward thrusts to force air out through the airway and dislodge the blockage. If the patient becomes unconscious, lay them down on the ground. Open the airway and manually remove the object if it is visible. If this is not possible, use chest thrusts and assess for CPR.

The chest thrust is similar to the abdominal thrust, but can be performed when the patient is lying down. It is also suitable in instances when the patient is pregnant or morbidly obese and the abdominal thrust is not possible. If the patient is standing, encircle their body with your arms and place a fist at the center of the sternum, issuing thrusts just as you would with a Heimlich maneuver. For supine patients, deliver upward thrusts to the middle of the sternum with the heel of the hand while kneeling beside the patient. When dealing with children over one year old, use the abdominal thrust for responsive patients. If the patient is unresponsive or becomes unresponsive during the abdominal thrusts, use chest thrusts, see if the obstruction is visible and can be removed manually, and begin CPR assessment if the obstruction persists.

There is a third technique for clearing airway obstruction which is helpful when dealing with adults, but essential in providing emergency care to infants: the back slap maneuver. In adults, the back slap is just what it sounds like and can be alternated with abdominal thrusts. With infants, it is important to angle the child downward to that their head is below their back. Rest them on a forearm to do so, making sure that the jaw is supported and no pressure is placed upon the throat. Deliver five hard slaps between the shoulder blades, stopping if the object is dislodged. After this, placed the other forearm on top of the child and turn them face-up, supporting head and neck in the process. Once again, if the patient becomes unconscious, visually check the airway and manually remove the obstruction if possible. If this has not removed the obstruction, then follow protocol for infant CPR.

Part 10: Circulation Assist Devices

In addition to manual CPR, a wide range of devices have been developed to assist compressions. These devices have a number of advantages, the first being that they maintain quality compression for periods longer than a single responder is able to maintain without assistance. The active compression-decompression device is a handheld suction cup which attaches to the chest in the center of the sternum. It assists decompression and improves venous return. This device has no contraindications and improves patient outcomes for adults with non-traumatic cardiac arrest.

Another circulation assist machine is the Impedance Threshold Device (ITD), a device placed between the ventilation source and a facemask or endotracheal ventilation tube. In cardiac arrest patients, there is not sufficient blood pressure to push the blood through the body. The ITD restricts the influx of air during decompression, decreasing intra-thoracic pressure and stimulating circulation. This device should not be used with patients with pulmonary hypertension, chest pain, shortness of breath, aortic stenosis, congestive heart failure, or dilated cardiomyopathy. It is critical to ensure that a tight seal is created between the device and lungs, or the effectiveness of the ITD is compromised. The ITD is an adjunct to other circulation assist devices and is not recommended for use with manual CPR.

The mechanical piston device is an automated chest compression machine. This device combines a piston and backboard. The piston is driven either by electrical or gas. The patient is placed supine on a backboard and the piston is attached over the thoracic region. Though it has not been shown to benefit patient outcome more than manual CPR, the mechanical piston device is helpful when there are other emergency duties for the responder to attend to. Another automated chest compression device is the Load Distributing band or vest (LDB). This device distributes compressive pressure across the thorax and can be used individually or as an adjunct to manual CPR.

Automated chest compression devices can provide consistent and quality compressions for longer periods, and are helpful in instances requiring prolonged retrieval. This helps to avoid responder exhaustion. It also allows safe performance of CPR compressions in confined spaces such as ambulances or aerial retrieval. In addition, mechanical CPR frees up personnel to attend to other duties and reduces the potential of interruptions to compressions. Finally, defibrillation pads can be placed under the piston or band, enabling defibrillation during compression. However, these devices should only be used in patients above 130kg and 18 years of age. They are not suitable for all body sizes, and should not be used for traumatic injuries. They may also shift out of position during use and have the potential to create patient trauma. In addition, the level of care provided by mechanical CPR is not greater than that provided by manual CPR, and it is more prone to technical difficulties.

Part 11: Special Conditions and Ongoing Education

One of the most critical special conditions to take into consideration prior to administering CPR is pregnancy. When dealing with a pregnant patient, it is critical to displace the uterus to the left prior to beginning compressions. This takes the weight of the child off the aorta and vena cava, reducing the risk of aortocaval compression. One way to shift the uterus is with a left lateral tilt. This places the supine body in an incline tilting the body to the left. However, if this is unavailable or unfeasible, the uterus can be manually shifted to the left. From the patient's right, place the palm of the hand against the raised upper portion of the abdomen and press it leftwards across the body, gently but firmly. If on the left side of the body, both palms can be placed behind the abdomen and the responder can pull the abdomen to the left. After this, CPR can be performed as per protocol for an adult. Make sure that no pressure is placed on the abdomen or the bottom tip of the sternum.

Opioids and opiates, including heroin, Dilaudid, Fentanyl, and Morphine, cause severe respiratory depression. A patient that has overdosed will be breathing shallowly or not at all. Other signs include pinpoint pupils and severely decreased levels of consciousness. Apneic patients or those breathing insufficiently will require immediate life-supporting attention. As an emergency responder, it's likely that the patients you encounter will have been in this condition for some time, which means that they need oxygen quickly. Check airway and begin rescue breaths immediately. If the patient lacks a pulse, then begin CPR.

Another potential treatment for opioid overdose is naloxone, a medication which restores the respiratory drive during an overdose. If nasal naloxone is available, use the needleless syringe to inject 0.5mL up each nostril. If using injectable naloxone, inject 1cc into a muscle after a few rescue breaths.

Continue rescue breathing for another two to three minutes. If there is no response, administer another 1cc. If the patient is not revived after a second dose, either their heart has stopped, in which case CPR is necessary, or the influence of the opioids is unusually strong and the patient requires more naloxone. Check local protocols to see if EMT's are able to administer naloxone.

If the patient does respond, be cautious. Patients awoken suddenly from an opioid high may be violent and combative. Also, patients may attempt to use again to eliminate the feelings of withdrawal, which will result in another overdose. Finally, if too much naloxone is administered, the patient may vomit violently and go into seizure. Make sure to maintain the airway if this occurs, and take care when administering naloxone to avoid this at all possible.

When resuscitating a patient, it is important to consider the family as well as the patient. Remain calm and communicate clearly with the family regarding the patient's condition. If enough team members are available, one responder should be assigned to communicate with the family. Their primary concern is to build rapport and provide updates, helping family members in crisis to handle the situation. This is critical in conditions when the emergency leads to death, especially when this death occurs on the scene. Direct and private communication with the family will help to provide all possible care and ease the pain of loss. Be sure to familiarize yourself with the psychological and medical impacts on the loved ones in times of emergency and how to best handle these impacts.

Best practice for CPR, as with all medical procedures, continues to evolve over time. Plus, it is vital to keep your skills up to date. Thankfully, there are a number of public resources available to enhance and refresh your CPR skills. Community classes also expand CPR knowledge and skills to others, increasing the likelihood that a qualified bystander will provide life-giving care in the event of an emergency medical event. This means that it is important for all responders to be active in CPR education in their community, both to keep their own knowledge fresh and to provide their expertise to others.

Section 3: EMS Operations

Remember that the EMT is one component of the EMS, or emergency medical system. To get the best patient outcomes, all parts of this system must work together like a well-oiled machine. Each part of the EMS system is governed by procedures and guidelines that help to coordinate rescue services. These guidelines outline the role and proper function of the EMT and other elements. In this section, we will explore all components of the EMS and discuss where the emergency responder fits in this system. We will also review the considerations necessary to ensure the health and proper function of the EMT.

Part 1: EMS Systems

Emergency medical services provide a coordinated response for emergency medical care. Often, those who are sick, injured, or experiencing other medical conditions require emergency care. If this is the case, then EMS systems allow the public to call for emergency responders. These responders then provide immediate life-saving care and stabilize the patient while on the way to the hospital. There are many levels of emergency care, from basic life support services to emergency room care at the hospital. EMS also includes a range of other personnel and equipment, as well as a level of training which facilitates the necessary responder response.

Ambulances are an essential part of this system, as they transport responders and equipment to the scene of the emergency and facilitate transport of the sick or injured patient to the hospital. Emergency dispatching coordinates these ambulances, ensuring that they arrive on scene as needed. Medical oversight refers to the supervision of a physician which reviews and directs the function of emergency responders. Responders also require certification and licensure. Certification ensures that they have the knowledge and skills necessary to perform their function, while licensure is determined by the state and ensures that EMTs are legally permitted to perform their scope of work as emergency responders. Licensure also ensures that each responder is well aware of the scope and limitations of their duties.

The National EMS Scope of Practice defines four levels of emergency response, each with its own role and scope of duties. These four levels are EMR, emergency medical responders, EMT or emergency medical technician, AEMT or advanced emergency medical technician, and paramedic. The knowledge base and skills requires for each level expands upon the previous. Also, each level of emergency response requires specific training, certification, licensing, and credentials. Finally, the American Disabilities Act of 1970 provides special provisions for EMTs with disabilities to perform EMS activities if they have the physical capacity to do so.

The most current mode of National EMS Scope of Practice was established in 2018 and defines the skills, certifications, and licensure required by each level of emergency response. EMRs, or emergency medical responders, are responsible for providing immediate life-giving care. They stabilize the patient and provide assistance to the EMTs once they arrive. EMRs are responsible for performing basic interventions with minimal equipment. Once the EMTs arrive, they provide emergency medical care and transportation. They function under medical oversight, providing more comprehensive emergency medical care, and ensuring that the patient is stable until they reach the hospital. EMTs are also certified and licensed to administer certain prescribed medications to a patient in times of emergency. EMTs require a 150 hour certification course to ensure that they can function adequately in the field.

Building on the skills and knowledge of the EMT< the AEMT, or advanced emergency medical technician, has the skills for advanced life support care. This requires an additional 200-400 hours of training and involves advanced techniques for the administration of medication, maintaining the airway, and using IV therapy. After this, continuing education can provide the certification and licensing to act as a paramedic. This requires intensive training ranging from 1000 to 1300 hours. Paramedic training covers advanced life support skills and paramedics function under medical oversight in the field. They are well-versed in all life-support equipment present in the ambulance and have all the credentials necessary to take all pre-hospital measures to provide pre-hospital care. Paramedics are the final link from the emergency scene to hospital care.

The coordination and organization of emergency medical services is a relatively recent innovation. The White Paper of 1966 made provisions for national organizations for accident prevention and the handling of emergency traumas. It also put measures into place which led to the national institution of 911 as an emergency number, as well as the institution of ambulances as a component of the emergency medical response system. The White Paper addressed many aspects of accident prevention and handling, including the creation of emergency rooms in hospitals and centralized collection of trauma data to enhance future emergency response. It also made provisions for government funding for EMS.

The White Paper also led to the development of the National Highway Transportation Safety Administration (NHTSA), which is charged with saving lives, preventing injuries, and reducing vehicle-related crashes. In the same year, and just following the National Traffic and Motor Vehicle Safety Act, Lyndon Johnson signed the Highway Safety Act, which put into place measures for enforcing safety in the construction of motor vehicles. Essentially, the establishment and refinement of EMS services owes its development almost entirely to the growing national awareness around highway-related deaths. The development of EMS services has continued over the last several decades, now focusing on public health and both primary and secondary preventions. Primary prevention is the prevention of an onset of a disease, while secondary prevention relates to the earliest possible detection. Public health is the effort to prevent disease, prolong life, and to promote health through the organization of public and private organizations. The EMS Agenda for the Future currently focuses on integrating emergency health care with the remainder of the health system, as well as making it reliable, accessible, and subject to constant evaluation.

The current EMS has fourteen components. These are: public access, communication systems, clinical care, human resources, medical direction, legislation and regulation, integration of health services, evaluation, information health systems, evaluation, system finance, education systems, prevention and public education, and EMS research. Public access provides a system to request help. By calling 911, a person in need can reach a public safety access point, an emergency medical dispatch (EMD) that can send responders to provide first aid and CPR. These communication systems permit the transfer of information by radio and other communication links, and they are divided into primary service areas to facilitate localized response. Modern communication systems use GPS to track the location of responders and patients, and wireless communications can transmit response maps and update information for responders.

The third component of the EMS is clinical care. This involves EMRs and EMTs trained to provide immediate care and use equipment within the scope of practice. EMRs and EMTs must also be capable of checking, maintaining, and operating all equipment in the ambulance. The fourth component of EMS, human resources, is also vital for this aspect of emergency services. Human resources ensure that all personnel are adequately trained and certified to handle patients and equipment. Another aspect is to ensure that all personnel are compensated for their services. The human resources component is also responsible for attracting quality and talented personnel and ensuring that they retain well-being and upward mobility in their career path.

The next vital component of the EMS system is medical regulation. Regardless of the level of emergency response training, it is critical that emergency responders are supervised by medical personnel with the skills necessary to ensure the EMRs and EMTs follow their scope of practice and have all skills necessary to ensure that they can function appropriately. The medical director ensures that the EMRs and EMTs follow the sixth component: legislations and regulations. These laws and regulations are established by the state EMS offices and provide oversight over individual policies and daily procedures, often guided by an advisory committee. This component also includes medical control, which is the supervision of responders by physicians both during and after the emergency itself.

The seventh component of EMS is the integration of health services. This coordinates pre-hospital care with care once the patient has arrived at the emergency room. This includes protocol for time-sensitive procedures such as those which deal with heart attacks and strokes. The eighth component, evaluation, provides oversight and guidance for this function. Evaluation provides feedback on the results of emergency response care, including the recognition of errors relating to improperly established rules or the lack of necessary knowledge or skill. The ninth component, information systems, integrate staffing, equipment, and training to improve planning in future EMS activities. This is supported by the tenth component: system finance. The government must fund the training and operation of emergency services to both document care and ensure the continued function of all aspects of the EMS.

From this point on, all aspects of the EMS are designed around enhancing future response to emergency. The eleventh component is education systems. This includes providing accreditation to emergency responders and ensuring that certification programs provide all the necessary skills to perform appropriately in the field. Prevention is the next step, item twelve on the list, and it centers around reducing the cost of healthcare and expanding knowledge regarding the causes of injury and illness in the community. The next step, the thirteenth component of EMS, regards informing the community about CPR and other life-preserving procedures. This also enhances the standing of EMTs in the community. Finally, the last or fourteenth component of EMS is research, which is oriented around refining future EMS activities based on previous results. This provides continuous quality improvement (CQI). Currently, these efforts are focused on mobile integrated healthcare (MIH), which assists low income and elderly patients to reduce the demands upon the EMS, and the National EMS Information System, which coordinates information gathering, sharing, and storage to improve current and future EMS efficiency.

EMTs have several roles within the EMS, in additions to knowing and maintaining equipment, and handling medical emergencies in accordance with their scope of practice. It is also necessary for the EMT to maintain a professional appearance and conduct themselves with respect, empathy, and integrity. Finally, EMTs are responsible for protecting patient privacy. The regulation which provides guidelines for patient privacy protection is the HIPAA, or Health Insurance and Portability and Accountability Act of 1996.

This act defines what is covered by privacy privileges and strikes a balance between privacy and the necessary provision of health-related information for healthcare providers.

Part 2: Workforce Safety and Wellness

In order for the EMT to perform their duties and support best patient outcomes, they must safeguard their own health as well. This is not simply a physical matter; health involves social and mental well-being as well. In the line of duty, the EMT encounters many threats to health and wellness. These include high-stress circumstances and potential exposure to pathogens and dangerous circumstances. To support their own wellness and health, the EMT must understand stress responses and healthy stress management. Maintaining overall wellness includes making sure that they have proper sleep, nutrition and exercise as well as a healthy work/life balance. This also involves avoid unhealthy coping patterns such as substance abuse.

EMTs are often exposed to pathogens in the line of their duty. These include infectious or communicable viruses and bacteria, or those which spread from one person to another. The first step is risk management. The CDC or Center for Disease Control and OSHA, the Occupational Safety and Health Administration, provides a set of risk management guidelines and precautions. These include immunization for communicable diseases, which are vaccinations that foster immunity to specific pathogens. Other precautions include proper hand washing, the use of gloves, personal protective equipment, needles and sharps injury prevention, cleaning and disinfection, waste disposal, and safe injection practices.

The second step is proper management after exposure. In the event of exposure and potential contamination, first clean the area and then follow the exposure control plan put in place by your department. This also involves reporting all exposure to the designated infection control officer with the proper paperwork. The officer will then act as a liaison between the emergency responder and medical personnel to address all remaining measures.

Depending on the nature of the exposure and the contamination, different measures are set in place for post-exposure management. In communicable diseases, an individual can house the bacteria or virus, acting as a host to spread this disease to others. Infection control involves understanding the transmission of a given pathogen. The transmission of a pathogen can occur through direct contact, in the event of blood borne pathogens such as the human immunodeficiency virus (HIV) or indirect contact as in the case of airborne, foodborne, vector-borne, or waterborne transmission. Vector-borne transmission is the spread of a virus or bacteria by insects.

In the line of duty, emergency responders are often called to scenes with a number of hazards, including contaminants, fire, traffic hazards. Scene safety is of the utmost priority at all times. The responder should assess the scene for all potential hazards. This includes noting safety placards and the following all hazard precautions in accordance with guidelines laid out in the Emergency Response Guidebook (ERG). In scenes involving projectiles, it is also important that the responder is well versed in cover and concealment, or the tactical use of an impenetrable barrier to protect EMS personnel from projectiles.

Another important aspect of scene safety is personal protective equipment (PPE). Different hazards require specific protective clothing. Helmets, gloves, cold weather gear, hearing protection, eye protection, and body armor are all potentially required for certain scenes. Other PPE which might be required on scene are turnout gear, such as that worn by firefighters in scenes with fire hazards, body armor for scenes involving violence, and high visibility vests on constructions sites and other sites requiring visibility. The responder should also be aware of the potential hazards of long hair and jewelry, especially in scenes involving machinery.

Moving on to the social and mental aspects of well-being, the responder should be well-versed in handling situations that involve critically ill patients, as well as those that are dying or with family and witnesses in the event of death. When a patient is critically ill, they will be under a great deal of stress. This can cause them to respond with depression, hostility, or anxiety. All patients should be handled with honesty, dignity, and respect. In many cases, this is more important than the medical treatment itself. When dealing with death, the patient and family members will undergo the grief response. There are five stages of grief: denial, anger, bargaining, depression, and acceptance. It is important for the EMT to anticipate these responses and communicate compassionately, empathetically, sincerely, and without judgment.

Another aspect of mental well-being is stress management. The EMT will often encounter high stress environments. It is important to understand the stress response, as excess stress can lead to insomnia, irritability, and mental fatigue. The typical response to stress is known as general adaptation syndrome. This has three stages: alarm response, reaction and resistance stage, and recovery or exhaustion stage. In the alarm stage the fight-or-flight responses of the body are triggered. This included increased heart rate as well as boosted levels of adrenaline and cortisol. If stress continues, the body enters the resistance phase and adapts to a higher stress condition. Blood pressure and stress hormones remain elevated. Other symptoms include poor concentration, frustration and irritability. If stressful conditions continue, the body enters a stage of exhaustion. Symptoms include decreased stress tolerance, anxiety, depression, burnout, and fatigue.

In situations of extreme stress or prolonged stress an individual can develop adverse reactions to stress and ongoing mental and physical conditions. Extremely high stress incidents can cause acute stress response. This is a psychological condition which results from experiencing or witnessing a traumatic event. The affected individual will often relive the event, experience, dissociating symptoms, and be in a state of anxiety and hypervigilance in response to trigger stimuli. Acute stress reaction can be extremely disruptive to normal function. If this reaction continues for more than four months, it is known as delayed stress reaction or post-traumatic stress disorder (PTSD). It has also been recognized that long periods of stress can result in a similar condition, called cumulative stress reaction. In order to mitigate the effects of stress, responders and patients are offered critical incident stress management (CISM) after a crisis situation.

Social management is also important in the EMS workplace environment, just as in all workplace environments. One pertinent issue relating to social management is the potential for sexual harassment. All organizations involved in the EMS should have policies in place governing workplace interactions so that employees have recourse in the event of inappropriate interactions. Similar guidelines should be in place to protect employees from harassment on the basis of cultural diversity, as diversity is continually increasing throughout society. Finally, it is important for policies to be in place regarding injury, illness, substance abuse, and suicide prevention. This is especially important in EMS, as employees face high-stress environments and lives depend on their capacity to function effectively.

Part 3: Legal, Medical, and Ethical Issues

The medical field covers a wide range of ethical and legal issues in addition to specifically medical concerns. All medical care should be given in accordance with the law and administered with respect for the patient's legal and ethical rights. There are also certain aspects of care which are legal requirements. In these instances, failing to provide adequate care constitutes negligence and the emergency can be charged accordingly. Therefore, it is critical for the EMT to understand all laws and ethical concerns surrounding emergency medical care.

The guiding ethical principle of the EMT is primum non nocere, first do no harm. The EMT code of ethics also includes doing all that is possible to preserve life, alleviate suffering, and promote health. The EMT is ethically bound to provide an equal quality of care to all and to never use their skills in a way detrimental to the public. Finally, EMTs are ethically bound to conduct themselves professionally and to respect the patient's confidentiality. The legal obligation of the EMT is the duty to act, assess, treat, and transport. This means to respond expeditiously and safely to calls, to thoroughly assess the scene and the patient, to provide appropriate treatment, and to provide transport to the appropriate receiving facility when it is warranted. These duties involve several medicolegal elements, or elements which involve both law and medical treatment.

One right of every patient is the need to give consent prior to receiving treatment. It is also important that this consent be informed, meaning that the patient is explained the possible consequences and all potential risks. If patients are competent, then they have the right to refuse care. This is patient autonomy, the right for patients to make decisions about their own health care. Health care providers may educate the patient, but may not make decisions for them. If it is possible, then express consent, or consent given verbally or in writing, should be obtained from the patient. If the patient is unable to consent because they are unresponsive or otherwise unable to provide express consent, but it is assumed that they would do so if they were able, then consent is implied. If a patient refuses care or transport, then they must be legally capable of giving consent, of sound mental faculty, and fully informed of all of the risks. They must also sign release forms which absolve the EMT of negligence for not giving care.

There are additional special conditions related to consent. If the patient is evaluated as lacking decision making capacity, and if it is reasoned that they would give consent if capable of making decisions, then implied consent is given. Another special condition is covered by the emergency doctrine. This states that individuals are allowed to take action in times of emergency, in the event that there is a sudden or urgent need for aid, without following normal standards of reasonable care. Involuntary consent may be obtained for individuals in the care of law enforcement officers or patients mandated into the care of mental health officials. In these instances, this can involve forcible restraint and treatment. Forcible restraint is also necessary at times with a combative patient that is at risk of hurting themselves or others. Medical control should be called prior to restraint, and most states require a law enforcement officer present as well. If this is not feasible, then a witness should be present to confirm the need for restraint.

Another area of consent which differs from the typical is in the treatment of minors. Minors are considered unable to give consent, and therefore it falls to the parent to consent to medical treatment. If the parent is absent, but there is another individual who acts as a temporary guardian for the minor, such as a schoolteacher, then consent may be obtained from this temporary guardian. In legal terms, they are acting in loco parentis, or in the place of the parent. If no guardian is available, then the child may be treated under the emergency doctrine, if their lives are in immediate danger.

The only time in which a minor can legally consent to care is if they have been emancipated. Emancipated minors have the same legal rights and obligations as adults. Additional patient rights include confidentiality and the right to establish a DNR or living will to specify their healthcare wishes when they are no longer able to physically do so.

Another important medicolegal issue regards death. Resuscitation should be administered to patients unless they exhibit definitive signs of death. Definitive signs include decapitation, putrefaction, rigor mortis, or dependent lividity. In these instances, medical examiners will often be on scene. A patient can also show physical and presumptive signs of death. Presumptive signs of death can be evaluated by a responder on the scene. They include lack of a carotid pulse or heartbeat, unresponsiveness of painful stimuli, a lack of corneal and deep tendon reflexes, an absence of breath sounds, a lack of systolic blood pressure, profound cyanosis, and lowered body temperature. Physical signs of death can only be determined by a physician. If there is any doubt, then the patient should be treated as if they were alive and resuscitation efforts should be begun.

If an EMT encounters an organ donor in the field, they should receive the same quality of care as anyone else. Even in the event of the patient's death it is important to keep the patient alive as long as possible, as the tissues will still require oxygen. Policies on organ donation are different from one area to another, so it is important for each EMT to understand the practices of their area. Tissue and organ donation can still happen after death in some areas. It is also important to check for medical insignia or medical bracelets. These will have important patient information which can have an impact on the course of treatment.

There are a number of medicolegal terms which relate to the care offered by the EMT. In all circumstances, it is the responsibility of the EMT to act within their scope of practice, which is the care, as determined by the state, which can be provided to a patient by an EMT. They must also provide the appropriate standard of care. The standard of care is the manner in which an EMT should act or behave to prevent further harm to a patient. This is influenced as well by the legal duty to act, which is the EMTs obligation to provide care to the patient. The duty to act is defined by law and departmental policy. Any failure to conform to these standards is considered negligence. The EMT is legally obligated to continue patient care until the patient can be transferred to another appropriate provider. It is also important that care not be forced upon a competent patient that has not given consent. It is also critical that the EMT provide accurate and honest disclosure of all pertinent information, as defamation can follow from any false or inappropriate disclosure.

There are other legal concerns that an EMT must be aware of. Each of the following situations are instances of a torts, a wrongful act, injury, or damage. If the EMT does not provide the level of care that another person in the same situation would reasonably provide, they are then guilty of negligence. If care is discontinued before the patient is transferred to an individual with equal or greater care, then they are considered guilty of abandonment. If the EMT unlawfully places a patient in fear of bodily harm, then they are considered guilty of assault. If they touch a person unlawfully, they are considered guilty of battery. If a patient is seized, abducted, confined, or carried away without their consent, then they are guilty of kidnapping. This can also be considered false imprisonment. Proximate causation is when an injury is deemed to have been caused by action or inaction on the part of the EMT.

In the event of an injury, they EMT can be considered guilty of negligence under the principle of res ipsa loquitur, Latin for "the thing speaks for itself". This means that negligence is assumed in the event of an injury even if there is no specific evidence of a negligent act. In these instances, the EMT must prove that the EMT acted in accordance to their duty and did not breach this duty. Hey must also be able to show that they provided the appropriate standard of care. There must be an injury for negligence to be charged under res ipsa loquitur. Negligence per se is when the EMT is alleged to have acted in violation of a statute. The EMT is also legally mandated to report suspected abuse or neglect, and to fail in this is also a case of negligence. Finally, if the patient breaches confidentiality, they can be considered guilty of slander, if the breach is verbal, and libel, if the breach is written. In each instance, the EMT can be brought up on criminal charges.

Although there are numerous legal pitfalls facing the EMT, there are some protective laws and measures as well. Good Samaritan laws have been passed by all states for the protection of EMTs following their duty to act and acting within the scope of duty. These laws provide immunity from prosecution in the event of injury or poor patient outcome. However, they provide a different degree of protection in each state. The greatest coverage provided by Good Samaritan laws provides for protection for everything up to gross negligence, which is intentional injury to the patient or willful, wonton, reckless care.

It is also important for EMTs to keep accurate and detailed records covering all patients.

These should be maintained in the event of legal proceedings or court appearances. If the EMT is brought up on charges, the goal of the court case is to determine whether or not the EMT has administered all patient care ethically. Ethics is considered the philosophy of right and wrong and the study of morality. In EMT terms, it is a set of social guidelines which governs social moral behavior. Morality, on the other hand, is a personal code of conduct defined by a person, religion, or society and influencing conscience, conduct and character. Bioethics is a field of ethics related specifically to health care practices. When this is related to the professional conduct of the EMT, it is known as applied ethics. This guides EMTs to act in the best interests of their patients and to conduct themselves professionally in accordance with their position. Furthermore, EMTs are expected to act according to precedence, or the guidelines, lessons, and rules obtained from previous experience.

If an EMT is brought up on charges, there are three elements which can aid their defense. These are contributory negligence, governmental immunity, and the statute of limitations. Contributory negligence is the claim that the plaintiff contributed in some way to the damages or injuries that they sustained. Governmental immunity is protection afforded to governmental or municipal EMS entities. This protects them from being sued or limits the amount of punitive damages that can be levied. The statute of limitations on these cases is three years, which means that after this time period has passed from the event, no case can be opened.

Cases of negligence often involve depositions, or oral questions asked of both parties while under oath, and discovery, a stage in which information is gathered to garner a better understanding of the case. The discovery phase may settle out of court instead of going to trial. If the responder is found guilty of negligence, the court may mandate compensatory damages, which are fined demanded from the defendant to cover the plaintiff's medical bills, pain and suffering, lost earnings, and damage to personal property. If the defendant has been found guilty of gross negligence, then they may be charged with punitive damages. These are fines in excess of actual damages which are charged in the event of willful or malicious misconduct.

Part 4: Documentation and Communication

The most important forms of documentation for the EMT are forms related to refusal of care and the PCR, or patient care report. Refusal of care should only be accepted from individuals deemed capable of giving consent, and they should be filled out and signed in the presence of a witness. The responder should make every effort to inform the patient about the treatment and the potential risks prior to accepting the patient's refusal of care. Each time patient care is administered, it is necessary to fill out a PCR. In most instances, different PCR forms are required for each different patient outcome. Details of transport and care should be reported, as well as an honest record of errors and the actions taken to correct them. Multi-casualty events should also be recorded as special situations.

Another critical aspect of EMS function is communication. Written forms constitute one aspect of communication between providers regarding a patient. When transferring care, and in preparation for the transfer, communication also takes place verbally in person, with phone, or over the radio. These communications are critical for coordinating all entities involved in the EMS. Radios are the primary means of communication between responders, hospitals, and dispatch centers. Telemetry is employed by these systems to convert electrical signals into coded audible systems.

Radio signals are also supplemented with cellular and computer communications, in the form of mobile data terminals (MDTs), pagers, and cellular telephones. However, cellular telephones are unreliable because, as with all repeater-based systems, they are useless if the equipment fails, is damaged, or loses power. Digital signals are used in paging and tone alerts because they can transmit faster and have more flexibility. Medical dispatch uses interoperable communications are making a wide range of different forms of communication are available so that no interruption in communication is experienced. It is the responsibility of all EMS personnel to ensure that all communication systems are maintained for the same purpose.

The central core of these communications is the base station, which is a fixed location containing a transmitter and receiver. The base station can be operated by a single individual speaking through a microphone, by telephone, or by radio through a communication center. Base stations usually have greater power than mobile units, and they can communicate with units at greater distances through more efficient antenna systems. The base station houses a repeater which receives messages on one frequency and transmits them on another.

The FCC, or Federal Communications Commission, regulates the use of radio communication in the US. The FCC assigns and licenses frequencies to specific agencies, facilitating efficient communication. Specific frequencies are called channels, and they are assigned to different purposes. Scanners search several frequencies until the message is completed. Channels dedicated to medical use are termed MED channels, and they include VHF (very high frequency) and UHF (ultrahigh frequency). UHF frequencies are short range, but have high penetration power and can pass through buildings. They are helpful in urban areas. VHF come in high band and low band, with high band travelling in a straight line and less susceptible to interference, but incapable of bending around the surface of the earth or around obstacles. Low band VHF follows the shape of the earth and travels around obstacles, but is more subject to interference.

Radios can be set in a number of ways, each changing how they function. Simplex radios receive and transmit on the same frequency, so that only one radio in the system can transmit at a time. Duplex radios receive and transmit on different frequencies, so radios in these channels transmit and receive simultaneously. Multiplex systems can transmit two frequencies simultaneously, permitting the responder to send ECG and voice communications at the same time. Systems can also be trunked, meaning that they use several frequencies and use a computer to route incoming communications to the next available frequency. Encoders are also used as a combination lock on a radio. A sequence of tones unlocks a particular radio so it can receive traffic intended for it while cutting out other traffic.

Radio communication is used to exchange information between the medical dispatcher and the emergency responder. These are two of the three modes of communication in the EMS, the third being the communication between the dispatcher and the party requesting help, which often takes place over a dedicated telephone line. The dispatcher reads pre-arrival instructions to the EMT to prepare them for the scene, including location, complaint, and other pertinent details. The responder then communicates to the dispatcher the unit ID and level of the provider, ETA to the hospital, sex and age of patient, their chief complaint, a brief pertinent medical history including major illnesses, assessment of the illness, the patient's vitals, the emergency care given, and the response to that care. All patient information should be reported accurately, objectively, and in a professional manner. The responder should also report special hazards, traffic delays, and road construction to the dispatcher.

If necessary, the responder requests medical direction from a physician at the receiving hospital. Medical control should be notified of the arrival of the incoming patient, to advise of special conditions, and to request advice or orders. They should also be contacted to guide the delivery of sophisticated care and to assist patients in taking medications. Medical control is responsible for guiding protocol, issuing orders, and performing post-call reviews. They can also issue standing orders, or instructions which can be followed as soon as it is possible to do so. During patient transfer at the hospital, the EMT should clearly and efficiently communicate the name of the patient, the chief complaint, additional pertinent medical history, additional treatment given during transport, additional vital signs taken during transport, and any changes since the last communication.

Another critical aspect of EMS communication is the therapeutic communication between the patient and the responder. The first element of this is to establish a rapport with the patient. This is done with verbal communication along with posture, body movements, and eye contact. Communication should also be adjusted to the patient's language abilities, functional age, or the patient's mental state, activity pattern, and ability to function in daily life, and their cultural background. Communication should also be modified in the event of patient disabilities such as hearing or visual impairment. The responder should place themselves at or below the eye level of the patient, use language they understand, use proper names, explain procedures before they are performed, be honest, and listen carefully to the patient's communication.

Effective communication requires competence, compassion, consciousness, and commitment. Ask open-ended questions leading to closed-ended questions to get a clear assessment of the patient's condition without missing pertinent details. The responder should respect the culture of the patient and avoid cultural imposition, in which their own cultural values are considered superior to those of others. Interpreters should be used, if possible, when communicating with patients that speak a different language. When handling deaf patients, speak slowly and carefully while facing them. In treating the elderly, give understanding, kindness, and patience alongside proper care. When communicating with children, get down to their level, be honest, try to keep it positive, and involve the adult.

Part 5: Patient Assessment

Assessing the patient is one of the most crucial aspects of the duties of the EMT. It begins with the dispatch call and continues until the patient is transferred. The assessment can be broken down into five phases: scene size-up, primary assessment, history, secondary assessment, and reassessment. When receiving the dispatch call, consider all information. This is the beginning of the scene size-up. Identify and ready the equipment and resources needed to deal with the specific emergency. Consider scene safety. Once arriving on the scene, assess it quickly for additional safety concerns for the responders, patient, and bystanders. Also try to determine the mechanism of injury or nature of the health emergency. Assess number of patients and whether or not additional resources are needed. Maintain situational awareness so that all changing circumstances can be adjusted to as necessary.

Primary assessment follows the scene size-up. This is a quick evaluation of the patient to determine life-threatening conditions. This includes checking vital signs and making sure that the patient is breathing, responsive, and has a pulse. Get an overall impression of the patient. Look for signs or symptoms of cardiac or respiratory distress. Check for spontaneous respiration, shallow breathing, labored breathing, retractions, nasal flaring, dyspnea, or the use of accessory muscles in breathing. Palpate the carotid to check for pulse. Also look for perfusion in the color of the child's skin and assess capillary refill. Check the patient's responsiveness with the AVPU scale, ascertaining if they are alert, responsive to voice, responsive to pain, or completely unresponsive.

This includes checking for mental orientation and altered mental status. The overall impression also involves checking for jaundice, frostbite, cyanosis, diaphoresis, distracting injuries, crepitus, which is a crackling, crinkly, or grating feeling under the skin, in the joints, or in the lungs, and DCAP-BTLS, which is an acronym that stands for: deformities, contusions, abrasions, punctures or penetrations, burns, tenderness, lacerations, and swelling. Patients in the tripod position may be experiencing respiratory distress. If resuscitation is necessary, first place the patient in the sniffing position, then issue compressions and breaths. Remember that the time immediately after a traumatic injury is known as the Golden Hour, the time during which prompt medical treatment or surgery is most likely to prevent the loss of life. The final step is to update all responding EMS units.

The next step in the patient assessment process is history taking. This is to gain a systematic account of all the patient's previous injuries, illnesses, and medical conditions. Also determine the history of the current conditions, all signs and symptoms, and the incident that triggered the emergency call. Use the SAMPLE framework to determine history. This means to check for Signs and Symptoms, Allergies, Medications, Past illnesses, Last oral intake or menstrual cycle (if pertinent), and Events leading up to the current illness or injury. Keep aware for pertinent negatives, or the lack of expected signs and symptoms, in order to refine the assessment. Medical history is often taken at the same time that the primary assessment is performed. Another helpful mnemonic for the history taking stage is OPQRST, which stands for: Onset (of pain or event), Provocation or Palliation (what makes it better or worse), Quality (how would the patient describe the pain), Region or Radiation (where is the pain, does it extend to other parts of the body, where and how far), Severity (on a scale of one to ten), and Time (of this event, previous events, including time of day or time of season for previous events).

The next step is secondary assessment, which is a more detailed evaluation of the patient to determine all additional conditions the patient is experiencing beyond those that are immediately life-threatening. This is a focused, head-to-toe assessment and should be performed only after the patient is stabilized. In cases of life-threatening primary concerns which require the responder's full attention, the second assessment may not be completed. The secondary assessment may also be done during transport if the patient requires immediate hospital attention. The secondary assessment is intended to locate the source of symptoms and begin management of the cause. It includes blood pressure, tidal volume, pulse oximetry and capnography, heart rate abnormalities, breath sounds, abdominal guarding, and auscultation. Pupils can also be assessed, remembering the PEARL mnemonic: Pupils Equal And Reactive to Light. When dealing with trauma patients, it is preferable to perform the secondary assessment prior to taking the patient's history.

Another useful tool for assessing patients is the GCS or Glasgow Coma Scale, which is used to assess the severity of brain dysfunction. The patient gets a score for Eye Opening, Verbal Response and Motor Response. For Eye Opening If the patient opens their eyes spontaneously they receive a 4. If they open their eyes to voice they get a 3. If they open their eyes to a painful stimulus they get a 2. If they do not open their eyes they get a 1. For verbal response if a person is alert to person, place , time and event they receive a 5. If they provide a confused response and are not alert to to person place time and event they receive a 4. If they say inappropriate words that do not make sense they score a 3. If they utter incomprehensible words or unintelligent noises they receive a 2. If they have no verbal response they receive a 1. Lastly for motor function if the patient obeys commands and has normal spontaneous movement they receive a 6. If they localize pain or withdraw to touch they receive a 5. If they withdraw to pain they receive a 4. For Decorticate (flexion) to painful stimulus they receive a 3. For Decerebrate (extension) response to painful stimulus they receive a 2. If they do not move they score a 1. The total score of Eye Opening, Verbal Response and Motor Response are added up to get the total GCS of the patient. The lowest possible GCS being 3 and the highest 15

The final stage of patient assessment, reassessment, requires a careful watch of the patient's vital signs. Stable patients should be checked every fifteen minutes, while unstable patients should be re-checked every five minutes. Monitor the patient's status to identify if it improves or deteriorates, and take note of what treatment causes these changes. Continue the patient assessment until the patient is transferred. During transfer, provide an accurate and concise report to the receiving personnel.

Part 6: Lifting and Moving Patients

It is essential to lift and move patients in the process of transport. There are several pieces of equipment that facilitate this movement. One of the most versatile pieces of equipment is the wheeled ambulance stretcher. This has the capacity to adjust to different heights and contains safety belts and features to navigate around corners and through tight spaces. The bariatric stretcher is similar to a wheeled ambulance stretcher, but has a wide wheel base to provide increased stability. An alternative is a backboard, a flat device used when the patient has a potential spine injury. The backboard, also known as a spine board or longboard, is used to immobilize patients to prevent movement around the spinal injury. They are equipped with handholds to lift the patient and straps to secure them. The short backboard is used for patients in a seated or semi-seated position suspected of injuries to the cervical spine.

The direct carry is used to transfer a supine patient directly from a bed to a stretcher. There are several forms of stretcher, including the portable stretcher, flexible stretcher, basket stretcher, used to carry a patient across uneven terrain inaccessible by vehicle, and the scoop or orthopedic stretcher which can be split into two or four pieces and then slid beneath the patient and clipped securely together to transfer a patient to a stretcher, longboard or vacuum mattress. It should be remembered that the scoop stretcher does not provide adequate immobilization to the patient's spinal column. The vacuum mattress is an alternative to the stretcher used to immobilize and transfer patients. It is especially useful in the event of limb, pelvis, or vertebra trauma, especially in the case of a trauma to the femur.

In some instances, the patient can be carried in a sheet. They should be centered in the sheet and the fabric on both sides of the patient should be rolled up tightly to act as cylindrical handles. Another device for lifting and moving patients is a stair chair. This can be used to transfer conscious patients that can be placed in a sitting position up or down stairs. The patient is strapped in with two straps, one placed across the torso, under the arms, and attached to the handles. Keep the head up and the feet down whether moving up or down the stairs. The Kendrick Extrication Device is a device used to extricate patients from vehicles in the event of traffic collisions. It keeps the head, neck, and torso in anatomically neutral position during extrication, thus reducing the likelihood of further injury.

Whenever moving a patient, it is important to use proper body mechanics to prevent injury to the provider and to avoid worsening the patient's condition. The patient should be kept as comfortable as possible, and care should be taken so that the patient is not dropped. The four principles of body mechanics are to: keep the weight of the object as close as possible to the body, contract the abdomen and use the legs, hips, and gluteal muscles to move heavy objects, stack the shoulders, hips, and feet, aligning them vertically, and reduce the distance and height that the patient must be moved, as much as possible. Avoid the swayback posture with the stomach bent forward and the buttocks extending anteriorly, also known as a lordosis. This will result in excess stress in the lumbar region. Also avoid kyphosis, which is a slouching position. This fatigues the lower back and increases pressure on the whole spine.

Use proper techniques to avoid injury to the responder or patient. When lifting, it is important to use the power lift, which both protects the patient and helps to defend the provider from injury. To do the power lift, bend at the knees and place the feet slightly outward, tightening the muscles of both the back and abdomen. Use the power grip, which is to place the hands at least ten inches apart with the palms facing up. Reaching and pulling can be a source of injury. When possible, reach no more than fifteen to twenty inches away from your body and push rather than pulling. However, avoid pushing the patient when the arms are fully extended.

When working with a team, coordinate all motions with clear communication and plan complicated moves prior to execution. In a two-person carry, the stronger person should be at the head, as 65-78% of a person's body weight is in their torso. Safe lift capacity for two people is considered 220lb. For a three-person carry, the third person should be behind the person at the foot to act as a spotter. Patients weighing more than 250lb should be moved with no less than four responders. The diamond carry is used with a backboard, with one person at head and foot and one person on each side of the torso, with carriers on head and side facing towards the feet of the patient and the carrier at the feet facing in the direction of movement away from the feet. This can be adapted to a one-handed carry with four or more responders. Use both hands for the lift and then release one hand, with carriers at the head and side turning towards the feet and the carrier at the head turning away from the feet in the direction of motion.

Moves can either be urgent or non-urgent. Urgent moves are performed when there is an immediate threat to life, while emergency moves are performed when immediate danger is present to the patient or responders. The urgent move is the rapid extrication technique, which is designed to move the patient in a series of coordinated movements from sitting position to a supine position on a long backboard and with a cervical collar. Emergency moves include the armpit-forearm drag, the shirt drag, and the patient drag. Non-urgent moves are performed when there is no immediate threat to life. The four types of non-urgent move are the direct ground lift, the extremity lift, the direct carry method, and the draw sheet method. The direct carry and draw sheet method are the primary methods for moving patients not suspected of having a spine, head, neck, or extremity injury to a bed or stretcher. The extremity lift is used for supine or seated patients not suspected of having injuries to the spine or extremities.

When working with geriatric patients, bariatric patients, infants, or combative patients, specific adjustments are necessary for lifting and moving. Geriatric patients are often fragile and susceptible to further injury. They also occasionally present the challenge of abnormal spine curvature, which can make it difficult to immobilize the patient on a long backboard. Bariatric, or obese, patients require special equipment, resources, and techniques, including bariatric stretchers, powered cots, and other devices to accommodate greater depth and bulk. When transporting young infants, it is necessary to use the neonatal isolette to keep the patients warm during transport. This also requires specialized training to operate. Finally, when dealing with combative patients that are in danger of harming themselves or others, it may be necessary to restrain them. Patient and staff safety is the first priority. However, prior to this, the patient should be evaluated to see if the combativeness has a correctable cause, such as head injury, hypoxia, or hypoglycemia.

Part 7: Transport Operations

The ambulance is a key aspect of the emergency medical system. It is a first-responder vehicle dedicated to the transport and short-term care of patients and designed to accommodate that purpose. Ambulances are designed according to KKK specifications and the NFPA 1917 Standard for Automotive Ambulances. They come in several types. Type I is built on a heavy truck chassis and used for advanced life support and rescue work. Type II ambulances are van-based with a raised roof. It is used for patient transfer and basic life support. Type III is also van-based but with a custom designed rear compartment and is used for rescue operations and advanced life support. All types include compartments for patients and drivers as well as warning and communication systems. Ambulances are marked with the Star of Life, which is a six-pointed blue star in a white field and featuring a white Rod of Asclepius in the center.

Each call has nine phases involving the vehicle and crew. These are: preparation, dispatch, en route to scene, arrival at the scene, patient transfer, transport, delivery, en route to station, and post-run. In preparation, the vehicle and all equipment within it should be inspected for proper function. This should happen before the call so that all equipment is ready when the vehicle receives dispatch orders. Dispatch must be available and staffed with trained personnel at all times. Dispatch relays to the responders the call location and the nature of the emergency. The ambulance then travels to the scene during the en route phase. The crew must be cautious regarding crashes or other roadway hazards. Seatbelts should be worn. If necessary, dispatch can be called to review and clarify information, and the team members should decide upon their relative roles on scene.

Once the crew has arrived on the scene, the ambulance should be parked safely while considering traffic considerations, patient access, and safe exit from the scene. The scene should be sized up, assessed for hazards, safety issues, and the need for additional resources. Patient care should be provided on scene as necessary, and then the patient should be transferred to the ambulance. All special equipment necessary should be used to transfer the patient safely to the ambulance stretcher. Proper transfer will depend on the specifics of assessment and treatment. Once the patient is successfully transferred, then the transport phase begins. Dispatch should be informed of the destination and time of departure. The receiving hospital should also receive a patient report, and the patient should be reassessed during transport. Transport should be done as quickly as possible, but in a way that avoids unnecessary risk to the patient.

Once the ambulance has arrived at the receiving hospital, dispatch should be informed of arrival. This is the delivery phase. The patient is brought into the hospital and transferred into the hospital bed and into the care of hospital personnel. A verbal report should be issued at this time, and charts should be completed. Next, the ambulance and all equipment should be deep-cleaned. This includes cleaning, decontamination, disinfection, high-level disinfection, and sterilization. Afterwards, it is time for the ambulance to return to the station. En route to the station, dispatch should be informed when the crew leaves the hospital. Local protocol might also require informing dispatch when the ambulance arrives at the station. On the way, refuel and get food if necessary. After the ambulance has returned to the station, the call enters the post-run phase. Jump kits should be restocked and all other equipment should be returned to the ambulance as necessary.

Perform maintenance and report any issues. Complete and file all paperwork. Complete full preparations so that the vehicle is ready for the next run.

Ambulance drivers must be fully versed in defensive driving techniques. Though ambulances in emergency mode are exempted from normal traffic laws, there is still the potential for accidents. Large vehicles with a high center of gravity must be handled appropriately. It is also necessary to use sirens and lights so that other drivers are notified. It is also essential to understand blind spots, the cushion of safety, and driver characteristics. The driver should also be aware of the dangers of excess speed, hydroplaning (at an excess of 30mph), and siren syndrome, which is the tendency for drivers to drive faster in the presence of sirens.

In extreme circumstances, helicopters and fixed-wing aircraft may operate as air ambulances. Medevac may be issued to call a helicopter directly to a scene. If this is done, then it is necessary to secure a landing zone.

Typically, the ideal landing zone size is considered to be 100ft x 100ft and on level ground. Safety around the landing zone is a primary concern. It should also be remembered that if the helicopter lands on uneven ground, then the rotors will be closer to the ground on the uphill side.

Part 8: Team Cooperation

The effectiveness of the EMS and of all modern healthcare is team interaction. And, in the case of any team interaction, collaboration and communication are vital. Care of the patient is transferred from the EMT to other members of the healthcare team. The approach guiding this is mobile integrated healthcare (MIH), which ensures a continuum of care which guides and tracks patients over time through a comprehensive array of health services spanning all levels and intensity of care. This healthcare model is also characterized by community paramedicine, which allows EMTs and paramedics to operate in expanded roles assisting primary healthcare and public health services with the underserved portions of the community.

Within the MIH model, there are different types of teams, including regular teams, temporary teams, and specialty teams formed for specific events. The advantage of a team is that it can include members with different specialties, offering multidisciplinary services to patients. Teams are distinguished from groups, which are composed of several healthcare providers all working independently to care for a single patient. Teams operate interdependently and have clear roles to coordinate their services. Teams are coordinated by a team leader tasked with making major decisions and directing the efforts of all team members. Groups may be dependent or independent. Dependent groups rely upon a single leader for direction. All members of an independent group make decisions within their area of responsibility. Groups can be organized according to the incident command system (ICS), which is a standardized approach to coordination, control, and command of the emergency response.

In order for a team to perform effectively, all members must have clear responsibilities and roles and operate together towards a shared goal. It is up to the team leader to facilitate the coordination and performance of the team and each team member should be encouraged to make perceived problems known and offer input. Essential for performance is crew resource management, which is a set of training procedures that make all roles clear and a foundation of communication, coordination, and clear decision making. Team performance also requires measures for troubleshooting and for addressing and minimizing conflicts when they occur. It must always be remembered that the first priority is the patient. Additional techniques for minimizing trouble and conflict include remaining calm, focusing on behavior, choosing battles, and waiting until after the incident to address any interpersonal problem actions or interactions.

Effective coordination is essential during the transfer of care, as this is a point where life-threatening errors can occur. The interruption of care during transfers should be minimized, and critical care should be completely uninterrupted by the transfer. Responsibilities must be transferred clearly and without confusion. This is facilitated by a standard format of transfer and common priorities. It is also necessary to pass critical information on to the next team member. The overall goal is for the transfer to result in minimal interference to patient care.

Another area which requires smooth and effective coordination is the interaction between Advanced Life Support (ALS) and Basic Life Support (BLS). ALS and BLS teams work with one another, and ALS continues as an extension of BLS, with some procedures and care overlapping. EMTs are typically responsible for BLS; however, they are often called upon to aid in ALS procedures. These procedures include saline locks, vascular access, advanced airways, esophageal intubation, direct and video laryngoscopy, gum elastic bougie, endotracheal intubation, and oxygenation, preoxygenation, and apneic oxygenation.

Part 9: Incident Management

One function of the EMS is to handle disasters and large-scale incidents. By their very nature, they require numerous teams and smooth interaction among them. Guidance and coordination is provided by the National Incident Management System (NIMS) and the use of Incident Command. NIMS is a framework of private and governmental organizations which cooperate in times of large scale emergency and mass-casualty incidents (MCIs). The goal is mutual aid response from all of the organizations involved, characterized by interoperability, flexibility, and standardization. The five principles of NIMS are: preparedness, communications, maintenance, resources, and command.

Incidents themselves are managed by Incident Command. This is a modular organization with five functional areas: Command, Operations, Planning, Logistics, and Administration and

Finance. Incident Command is a single unified command system under the control of an Incident Commander (IC). The Incident Command System (ICS) also employs a public information office (PIO), liaison officer, safety officer, and Joint Information Center (JIC). It acts as a command past with clear lines of authority, a manageable span of control for all officers, and common terminology to facilitate clear communication. The Incident Commander establishes an incident action plan to coordinate separate organizations and other resources, essential to contract freelance organizations and task them with certain duties during the incident. While the incident is still ongoing, it is known as open. The situation is still unfolding and it is possible that further patients will be discovered. When the incident is closed, it is in a state of cleanup, where all initial disaster has passed and it simply remains for the patients to be treated and transported. Once the incident has passed, the Incident Commander gives the order for termination of command and the forces are demobilized.

It is essential for EMS organizations to have disaster plans based on likely hazards and mutual aid agreements with neighboring organizations. Both planning and preparation are essential for effective performance during the incident. This means that all personnel should have basic incident command training as well as interagency training in simulated responses. Incident Command has a medical branch which is further subdivided functionally into staging, transportation, treatment, and triage units. In some instances, rescue, special extrication, and morgue units may be added. Supervisors will be established for each unit to guide and coordinate efforts. Areas will be established for both treatment and transportation. In the treatment area, patients will receive treatment in the field. In the transportation area, ambulances and crews are gathered to transport patients receiving hospitals.

For EMS, a mass casualty incident (MCI) is any incident which stresses the capabilities of the EMS system. This can be any situation with three or more patients, or any situation with the potential to become an MCI. Command and triage should be initiated if an MCI occurs. In triage, patients are gathered in a casualty collection point and assessed as to the severity of their injuries. Different treatment areas are set up on the basis of severity, and the patients are issued color-coded triage tags which indicate the category of injury level. Primary triage is intended to categorize patients quickly and determine priority. Secondary triage is used in the treatment area to re-triage the patients and reassess the severity of their injuries. START triage refers to Simple Triage and Rapid Treatment and assesses the patient's ability to walk and their respiratory, hemodynamic, and neurological status. JumpStart triage is a variation upon START triage intended for triaging children in disaster situations.

One important aspect of scene safety is the presence of hazardous materials. Containers holding hazardous materials are marked with DOT placards. This includes transport vessels, bulk storage containers, non-bulk storage vessels, drums, intermodal tanks, and secondary containment areas. A crucial aspect of EMT training is to understand the various hazards and the safety placards that identify them. Material Safety Data Sheets (MSDS) will be present in the bill of lading of transport vessels. They will indicate the nature of the materials, their toxicity, and recommendation to address spills. If these materials are on scene, the scene becomes a HazMat incident. The EMT must recognize the nature of the incident and request the appropriate additional resources. The Chemical Transportation Emergency Center (CHEMTREC) should be contacted in the event of such a disaster. Authorities will set hot, warm, and cold zones around the spill to determine the level of exposure present in each, and a decontamination area will be established to treat exposure patients as they are rescued from the hot and warm zones.

Part 10: Vehicle Extrication and Special Rescue

Without additional training, special rescue will be beyond the scope of the EMT. Extrication, or the removal of a patient from entrapment, such as in a vehicle after a collision, requires coordination and communication between qualified personnel and is conducted around the EMT. On these scenes, safety is of the utmost importance. Proper PPE may include protective gloves, turnout gear, high visibility clothing, and helmets, depending on the nature of the incident and the specific hazards present. In the case of vehicle extrication, downed power lines should be treated as if they are all live, and cars containing patients should be stabilized. In addition to the hazards presented by other vehicles on the highway, airbags and shock-absorbing bumpers may also pose a threat to rescuers. Airbags are often present in the front of the vehicle and side-impact airbags are present on the sides. If they have not deployed during the collision, then it is possible that they will deploy at any time during the rescue operation. Shock-absorbing bumpers may suddenly release and spring back, injuring rescuers that stand too close. It is important to understand these hazards so that safety precautions can be made on scene.

The role of the EMT in extrication is to stabilize and package the patient while operating safely on the scene so that no further injury arises to the patient or the responders. It is also critical to maintain good communication during the dangerous and complex process of extrication. Extrication itself has ten stages: preparation, en route to scene, arrival and scene size-up, hazard control, support operations, gaining access, emergency care, removal of patient, transfer of patient, and termination. It is important to make sure that the vehicle or other area of entrapment is stable and that other hazards have been eliminated before attempting extrication. If this is impossible and danger is imminent, rapid extrication is a last resort. The goal is to gain access. Simple access means that access does not require specialized tools, while complex access means that specialized tools are required.

Special rescue situations may also happen in the event of collapsed buildings, fires, water rescue, search and rescue, and SWAT situations. These are all technical rescue situations, and each situation has unique safety concerns. Specialized weapons and rescue (SWAT) teams will be called out in tactical situations. Responders should wear body armor and other suitable protective gear, and they should be familiar with the use of cover and concealment. Water rescue will require the use of scuba (Self-Contained Underwater Breathing Apparatus) equipment. Structure fires will require cooperation with fire control teams. In all situations, communication and safety are the first priority.

Part 11: Terrorism and Disaster Response and Management

Terrorism is a violent act intended to instill fear. The target of these acts is often civilian, and the act itself is designed to instill fear. These hazards can happen anywhere and at any time, and they can either be conducted against single targets, organized groups, or multiple indiscriminate targets. They can be done by those within the country, in the case of domestic terrorists, or from those outside the country, in the case of international terrorists. In some instances, terrorism is state-sponsored, meaning that rival governments provide funding for international terrorist activities. Given that the rate of terrorist attacks has increased, it is important for EMTs to be prepared to handle these incidents if they occur. In recent times, this has included mass shootings and the Boston Marathon bombing.

Terrorist acts can happen in a number of forms. One of the most feared is the weapon of mass destruction (WMD), also known as the weapon of mass casualty (WMC), as the intention of these devices is to create a large amount of casualties. These devices can take a number of forms: explosive, chemical, incendiary, nuclear, or biological. The acronym used to remember these devices is B-NICE. Terrorists have preferred the use of explosives, though all have been employed by terrorists except for nuclear devices. Dirty bombs are explosives loaded with radioactive material that add radioactive contamination to explosive damage. Weaponization is the process performed to artificially maximize a target population's exposure to a biologic agent to produce the highest number of casualties.

Since there are so many different types of devices that may be used in terrorist activities, the EMS response must be adjusted to the specific nature of the attack. It is important to know the appropriate response for each situation. Terror attacks are covert, meaning that they occur without forewarning. In mass casualty incidents, it is also important to avoid cross-contamination, or the contamination that occurs by coming into contact with an agent as a result of coming into contact with another contaminated person. Another important concern in terror attacks is the possibility of a secondary device, or an additional explosive set to go off after the initial bomb.

Liquids or gases that are dispersed in the air to infect, injure, and kill are known as chemical agents. They come in a variety of forms, including cyanides, nerve agents, choking agents, and vesicants. Only cyanide and nerve agents have antidotes. Treatment for other chemical attacks is based only on the symptoms. A key concept of the chemical attack is persistency or volatility, which is the length of time a nerve agent will remain on a surface prior to evaporating. A key mnemonic to assess organophosphate poisoning is SLUDGEM: salivation, lacrimation, urination, defecation, gastrointestinal upset, emesis, and miosis. Another key concept is LD50, or the chemical dose which will kill 50% of the population. Each chemical agent has unique symptoms and treatments, so it is important to review all agents well.

Biologic agents include viruses, bacteria, and neurotoxins, and all three can be spread by multiple routes. Dissemination can occur through mail or by being released into food, water, or, in the case of airborne biological agents, simply by being released into the air. Bacteria and viruses are extremely dangerous, as they can be contagious and their incubation period and initial similarity to other illnesses can make them difficult to detect. Syndromic surveillance is used to monitor the potential for biological agents or outbreak. This surveillance is the monitoring of patients presented to emergency departments and alternate care facilities by local or state health officials, as well as the recording of the use of over-the-counter medications and EMS call volumes.

An important concept is the disease vector, or an animal that carries the disease and spreads it to other animals. In the event of an outbreak or biological attack, points of distribution (PODs) are established strategically for the mass distribution of antibiotics, antidotes, vaccinations, and other medicines and supplies. Neurotoxins cannot be spread from one person to the next. Viruses cannot be treated with antibiotics. Just as with chemical agents, each biological agent has unique signs and symptoms, and it is important to be able to recognize these in the field and to know the appropriate treatment.

Radiologic and nuclear devices emit radiation, an energy resulting from radioactive decay. Forms of radiation include neutron, gamma, beta, and alpha, each with a different penetration potential. The extent of radiation exposure from a radiated source is lessened by distance, time, exposure, and shielding. Nuclear explosive devices can be put in the form of Special Atomic Demolition Munitions (SADM), which are small suitcase-sized nuclear weapons intended to destroy individual targets. Radiological dispersal devices are containers designed to disperse radioactive material. The degree of harm caused by radiation is based upon the exposure time and the intensity or the RADs of the radiated source. It is important for EMTs to be familiar with the signs of radiation sickness and the treatment measures employed for various degrees of exposure.

Incendiaries and explosive devices are some of those most commonly used by terrorists. Incendiaries cause fires, while explosive devices use explosive energy to cause injury, damage, and death. These can come in any size, from mail bombs to backpack bombs to truck bombs. Most often, they are in the form of IEDs, or improvised explosive devices. When responding to an explosion, it is important to be aware that terrorists often set up a secondary device to cause additional explosions.

Pulmonary blast injury is common with primary blast injury, which is the blast of high pressure. With pulmonary blast injury, the patient will show signs of apnea, tachycardia, and hypotension. The resulting ventilation/perfusion mismatch and acute respiratory distress syndrome (ARDS) will result in severe hypoxia. Supplemental oxygen will be necessary. Secondary blast injury is the result of projectiles. Tertiary blast injury is the result of quickly travelling wind. Quaternary blast injury is the result of burns, asphyxia, and exposure to toxic inhalants.

Section 4: Medical and Obstetrics/Gynecology

The two main types of emergencies that an EMT is called to respond to are medical emergencies and trauma. Trauma is an injury due to force exerted on the body, while a medical emergency may be something like a stroke or asthma attack, anything medical beyond trauma itself. This section focuses on medical emergencies. These come in a wide range of different forms, and to handle them properly requires an understanding of the entire range of human anatomy and physiology. Remember that this section is an outline of the major topics necessary to understand to effectively treat the varied forms of medical emergencies. It should be used as a supplement to the information found in your text on the subject.

Part 1: Types of Medical Emergencies and Common Treatment

Medical emergencies can be classified according to the system of the body that they affect. Each type of emergency has its own causes, signs, symptoms, methods of treatment, and difficulty of management. The most immediate medical emergencies are cardiovascular and respiratory, and these have been described in the first two sections of this text. Other types of emergency include gynecologic, psychiatric, hematologic, endocrine, gastrointestinal, immunological, and neurological. The most common medical emergencies include breathing difficulties, collapsing, an epileptic fit or seizure, severe pain, heart attack, and stroke.

The first step in determining the exact nature of the medical emergency is to do a patient assessment. This has been described in the previous sections, and consists of the scene size-up, primary assessment, medical history, secondary assessment, and reassessment. In the event of a medical emergency, the goal is to evaluate the symptoms to determine the nature of the illness. IN the event of a medical emergency, this often requires a focused medical history assessment, which is a medical history evaluation that emphasizes the most likely causes to the specific medical event. A key concept in assessment is the index of suspicion, which is the evaluation of symptoms to form a first impression of the likelihood of a particular medical cause for the event. A high index of suspicion means that there is a strong possibility that the suspected medical condition is the cause of the medical emergency.

After completing the patient assessment (and during the assessment in cases that pose an immediate threat to life) the next steps are patient management and transport. In cases that do not pose an immediate threat to life, the time on scene should be minimal so that the patient can be rapidly transported to the hospital. The scene time is the time between the arrival of the responder on scene and the departure of the responder to the receiving hospital. Management depends entirely upon the symptoms presenting and employer policies. It may include airway management, CPR, medication, or other life-saving interventions.

Once it is certain that the patient has been stabilized sufficiently for transport, they should be packaged in the ambulance and delivered to the receiving hospital. At this point it is important to understand the level of priority. When patients are relatively stable, they are low-priority transport and can be conducted to the hospital without lights and sirens. This is considered safer. If the patient is experiencing life-threatening conditions where even a minute can make the difference between life and death, then lights and sirens should be used and they should be transported to the hospital as quickly as possible given current conditions and without risking their safety. The delivery point is the emergency department (ED) best suited to the patient. In most instances, this will be the closest receiving hospital. However, if the patient is in urgent need of specialized care that can be provided by a specific emergency department, it may be necessary to route patient transport to this destination instead.

When encountering infectious diseases, the EMT must take measures to avoid exposure and prevent cross-contamination. This requires special precautions and a clear understanding of disease transmission. Diseases present with a wide range of signs and symptoms which require intensive study to recognize and diagnose properly. In addition, the EMT must be familiar with the appropriate handling and treatment of contagious patients.

The same methods are used to assess patients with infectious diseases as are used for patients experiencing other medical emergencies.

Scene size-up, primary assessment, taking history, secondary assessment, and reassessment protocol should be followed. By taking note of the symptoms presented, the responder is better able to tailor the initial treatment to the patient's needs. Common symptoms include vomiting, fever, altered level of consciousness (ALOC), and dyspnea or shortness of breath (SOB). If you have encountered an infectious patient, sterilization and decontamination is of the utmost priority during the cleanup phase after treatment.

One possibility when encountering contagious diseases is that of a pandemic or epidemic. An epidemic is a widespread occurrence of infectious disease within a community (beyond what is expected), while a pandemic is a global outbreak. Sterilization of medical equipment, proper disposal of needles, and the effective use of personal protective equipment are necessary precautions to avoid spreading the infection further.

Some of the commonly encountered infectious diseases include HIV, herpes, hepatitis, influenza, tuberculosis, and meningitis. It is important to know the routes of transmission for each disease. The herpes simplex virus, for example, is contracted through close physical contact with a carrier, or an individual infected with the virus. Hepatitis has multiple routes of transmission, including blood, contaminated food, and sexual contact. Influenza can be transmitted through close contact, through droplets, such as those ejected with an unprotected sneeze, and in serious cases can be airborne. Meningitis is spread through respiratory or throat secretions, and generally requires close contact. HIV spreads through blood or sexual contact. Whooping cough spreads through droplets or contact with throat or nasal discharges. Tuberculosis is carried in airborne particles. Understanding how they are transmitted helps the responder to avoid contamination and reduce the spread of the disease.

With the wonders of modern technology come global travel, not just of people, but of the bacteria and viruses they carry. Because of this, there are global issues regarding infectious disease with which every EMT and medical professional should be aware. There are many thousands of pathogens or infectious bacteria and viruses, so many will require further study. However, two that each EMT should be familiar with are ebola and Middle East respiratory syndrome coronavirus (MERS-CoV). Ebola has symptoms of fever, fatigue, and diarrhea. Transmission occurs through blood and other bodily fluids, and patients should be fit with a facemask to prevent the spread. MERS-CoV was first discovered in Saudi Arabia but has been discovered in Europe and the United States. Symptoms include cough, muscle aches, fever, and diarrhea. If patients present these symptoms, it is important to ask about recent international travel to see if this disease is a possibility.

Part 2: Medical Terminology

A strong grasp of medical terminology is crucial for EMTs and other medical responders to communicate with physicians, the receiving hospital, and receiving personnel during transfer. Medical terminology uses prefixes and suffixes to modify a root word. The root word is the foundation, describing the main issue or area of the body. Prefixes often describe location within the body, while suffixes describe the condition affected that area. By studying the lists of medical prefixes, suffixes, and roots, it will be easy to identify words with familiar parts even if the word itself has not been previously encountered.

Medical terminology is also full of a number of acronyms, symbols, and abbreviations. They act as a form of shorthand, permitting complex information to be communicated without needing long complicated words. These are particularly important in documentation, as they can be written quickly and accurately convey a complex meaning. However, it's important to remember that certain agencies use different abbreviations, acronyms, and symbols than others. Make sure to familiarize yourself with those used by your agency and those with which you will communicate so that you can use approved notations in your documentation.

There are also a number of medical terms which pertain to the body and to motion. It is important to understand these so that areas of the body, regions of a limb, and types of movement can be described accurately and with few words. Some key terms are lateral and medial, anterior and posterior, proximal and distal, superior and inferior, and lateral and medial. Each of these is an antagonistic pairing, two words with opposite meanings. Medial describe the part of a joint or limb that is closest to the midline of the body, while lateral describes the part that is furthest from the midline. Superior means closer to the head, while inferior is closer to the feet.

Anterior is towards the front or ventral portion of the body, while posterior is towards the back or dorsal portion of the body. Proximal and distal are often used with limbs, and they describe the part closer to the point of attachment or center of the body (proximal), and the part further from it (distal). The apex is the tip of a rounded or pyramidal structure like the lungs or heart. Superficial is a term meaning closer to the surface, and it is often used as a description for shallow lacerations or cuts. Flexion and extension are words that describe motion, with flexion reduction the angle between parts of a limb, while extension increases the angle between parts.

Part 3: The Human Body

Another crucial area of knowledge is anatomy and physiology, the understanding of the structure and function of the human body. The body contains a number of systems, each of which is vital to health, and each of which prone to specific diseases or dysfunctions. Understanding these systems both facilitates understanding of signs and symptoms and the capacity to communicate with medical personnel. The first important aspect of anatomical terminology is topographical, the division of the body into different places. These planes facilitate quick and clear description of symptoms and injuries.

The coronal or frontal plane divides the body into posterior and anterior portions. The axial or transverse plane divides the body from bottom to top. The median or midsagittal plane divides the body into left and right sides. Other sagittal planes divide the body into right and left, but are not oriented along the midline of the body.

The structural foundation of the body is the skeletal system. This is composed of bones, ligaments, tendons, and cartilage. Ligaments link one bone to another. Tendons link muscles to bones. Cartilage cushions the meeting points of bones and joints, and provides structure for softer protrusions like the nose. The skeleton system is divided into the axial and appendicular skeleton. The axial skeleton provides the structure of the center of the body, including the skull or cranium, facial bones, thoracic cage, and vertebrae. The thoracic cage includes the ribs and sternum, the bones which protect the thorax, or the portion of the body between neck and abdomen.

The vertebrae are a series of small bones, individually called vertebra, that encircle and protect the spinal cord. The appendicular skeleton includes limbs and pelvis. The pelvis is the large bony structure supporting the contents of the abdomen and providing an attachment point for the legs. The thoracic cage, similarly, provides an attachment point for the arms. In the legs, the femur is the bone between hip and knee, the strongest bone in the human body. The tibia is one of the bones between knee and ankle, commonly called the shin bone.

The skeletal system and muscles together form the musculoskeletal system. This provides form and structure for the body, protects the vital organs, and facilitates motion. The muscles responsible for motion are the skeletal muscles, the muscles attached to the bones via tendons. Smooth muscles are attached to the intestines and blood vessels. There is a third form of muscles, the cardiac muscles. The smooth and cardiac muscles are involuntary, while the skeletal muscles are voluntary. The cardiac muscles are unique, similar in some ways to both smooth and skeletal muscle tissue, with contraction initiated and regulated through the pacemaker cells in the heart.

The respiratory system has been described in detail in the first section. It consists of the lower and upper respiratory system. The upper respiratory system is composed of trachea, larynx, pharynx, mouth, and nose. The upper portion of the pharynx, the portion behind the soft palate and connected to the nasal cavity, is termed the nasopharynx. The trachea is protected by a cartilaginous sheath known as the thyroid cartilage. The upper airway warms and humidifies the air prior to entry into the lower airway. It also contains the epiglottis, a flap of skin which hangs down from the back of the throat and reduces the risk of food entering the throat and lungs.

The lower respiratory system is composed of the lungs, bronchi, and bronchioles. Surrounding the lungs is the pleura, a tissue that lubricates the motion of the lungs and aids the optimal function of the lungs. The overall function of the respiratory system is ventilation, the movement of air in and out of the lungs, and respiration, which is the exchange of oxygen and carbon dioxide in the alveoli of the lungs. The main muscle responsible for the movement of air through the respiratory system is known as the diaphragm.

The circulatory system has also been described in detail in a previous section. It is composed of the heart, arteries, veins, and capillaries. There are two portions of the circulatory system: pulmonary, which pumps deoxygenated blood through the lungs to receive oxygen, and the systemic circulation, which pumps oxygenated blood through the rest of the system. The muscle of the heart is known as the myocardium, and it has special characteristics described in detail in section two. The heart itself has four chambers, a right and left atrium and right and left ventricle. The right chamber of the heart supports pulmonary circulation, while the left chamber supports systemic circulation. The atria collect a sufficient volume of blood from the venous return and channel it into the ventricles. The ventricles contract to pump blood through arteries. Capillaries are hair-thin divisions that permit the perfusion of blood to the tissues. Other significant terms are the stroke volume, which is the volume of blood pumped from the left ventricle in each contraction, while the cardiac output is the total amount of blood pumped by the left ventricle each minute.

The nervous system transfers chemical and electrical signals through the system to coordinated bodily function, sense stimuli, and trigger muscular contraction. It includes the nerves, spinal cord, and brain. The spinal cord and brain compose the central nervous system, while the nerve outside the brain and spine form the peripheral nervous system. Together, they coordinate blood pressure, breathing, temperature, and all other activity of the body and organs. The autonomic nervous system directs involuntary activities, while the sensory nervous system directs functional actions through the motor nerves. The sensory nerve channel sensory stimuli to the brain. The brainstem is the central trunk of the brain and consists of the medulla oblongata, pons, and midbrain and connecting to the spinal cord. It conducts messages between the brain and the rest of the body, controlling basic bodily functions.

The digestive and excretory system is responsible for breaking down food so that nutrients and calories can be absorbed into the bloodstream. It consists of hollow organs of the alimentary tract such as the esophagus, stomach, and small and large intestine. The solid organs associated with the digestive system are the spleen, pancreas, and liver. The oral cavity is the entrance to the alimentary tract. It contains salivary glands that release saliva, which contains salivary amylase, which begins the process of breaking sugars down. The stomach secretes acids which continue to break down foods, creating chime, a pulpy, acidic fluid which then passes into the small intestine. The liver secretes bile which travels through the bile ducts to enter the duodenum, the first section of the small intestine. Bile facilitates the digestion of lipids. Another key term is retroperitoneal, which refers to areas or organs outside of the peritoneum, the tissue that lines the abdominal wall and covers most of the organs in the abdomen.

The urinary system is responsible for eliminating waste materials from the body, maintaining the proper pH of the blood, and controlling fluid balance. It is composed of the two kidneys, the ureters, bladder, and urethra. The kidneys filter the blood and channel waste products to the bladders through the urethra. The urethra is the route for eliminating urine from the bladder. At low flow rates, the urine is driven through the urethra through peristalsis, which is the rhythmic contraction of circular muscles around hollow organs. As a side note, peristalsis is also responsible for moving material through the esophagus and intestines. Another key area in the urinary system is the renal pelvis, which acts as a funnel for urine from the kidney into the urethra.

The lymphatic system is responsible for holding lymph, the fluid in the body outside the circulatory system, and channeling the lymph fluid through the body. It is critical for supporting the circulatory and immune systems. Lymph serves a number of functions. It removes waste and toxins from the body, absorbs fatty acids, transports white blood cells, and helping to remove fluid from the tissues. This system consists of the lymph nodes, lymph vessels and glands, spleen, and thymus glands. The lymph nodes themselves are responsible for housing B and T lymphocytes and filtering foreign particles and cancer cells from the interstitial fluids.

The reproductive system contains the organs responsible for reproduction, or the production of new life. Reproductive anatomy is dimorphic, which means that different adult anatomical structures exist in males and females. For females, the reproductive organs include ovaries, fallopian tubes, cervix, uterus, and vagina. The ovaries produce eggs, which then travel through the fallopian tubes to the uterus. The lower opening of the uterus is known as the cervix. In males, reproductive anatomy includes the penis, testicles, and prostate gland. The sperm is produced in the testicles and travels through seminal vesicles to the penis during ejaculation. The prostate gland surrounds the neck of the bladder and releases a fluid which nourishes and protects sperm.

Central to diagnosis is pathophysiology, which is the effect that a disease has on normal physiological function. In the course of duty, an emergency medical responder will encounter diseases and conditions that impact different anatomical systems. Conditions that interfere with the proper function of the respiratory system will cause respiratory compromise, a lack of sufficient oxygenation which can be caused by any number of conditions which impact ventilation, oxygenation, respiration, or perfusion. Shock is another condition which requires a strong grasp of pathophysiology to treat properly. Shock results from a lack of blood flow and oxygenation. It is common after serious injury and can be caused by any disease or event. Symptoms include a drop in blood pressure and urine output, an increase of acidity in the blood, and lowered oxygen and circulating carbon dioxide levels. Immediate treatment includes elevating the legs and lowering the head to improve circulation to the brain, adding supplemental oxygen, warming the patient with a blanket, providing fluid replacement and medications to improve heart function, and treating the underlying condition promptly.

Part 4: LifeSpan Development

Medical emergencies can happen to anyone, of any age. However, at certain ages, we are more likely to experience certain medical emergencies. Therefore, it is important to understand the life span, the changes that happen from birth to death. This helps to diagnose and treat patients of any age accurately and promptly. Babies are called neonates in the first month after birth. From one month to a year, they are known as infants. Babies tend to have higher heart and respiratory rates than adults, and the younger the baby, the faster the rate. With regard to respiration, babies tend to have more flexible, though smaller airways. This makes them more vulnerable to airway obstruction via the aspiration of foreign objects. It should also be noted that babies tend to breathe through the nose, and that the spaces between their cranial bones has not yet ossified completely, leaving fontanels or soft spot.

Children from one to three years of age are known as toddlers. They commonly experience separation anxiety, and their language development is variable. Between three and six years old, they are known as preschoolers. Their respiratory and heart rates will be faster than adults but slower than infants. Accidents are common in these children, and it is not uncommon for them to experience airway obstructions as well.

From six to twelve years old, children are considered school-age. Language is often sufficiently developed, so it is important to explain the necessary procedures. This will help to reduce anxiety and fear, allowing treatment to be offered more promptly and effectively. It should also be remembered that children of this age have begun to enter conventional reasoning stage, which means they tend to look to peers and society for approval. Prior to school age, children tend to be motivated by preconventional reasoning, which is the idea of punishment and reward.

Between thirteen and eighteen years old, children are considered adolescents. Once children reach this age, they are treated medically just as adults are treated. However, their size may be considerably less than adult size, which means that medication and certain treatments should be adjusted accordingly. The most common cause of death for adolescents is accident.

From 19 to 40, people are considered early adults. During this time, individuals are at their physical peak. As the individual comes to the end of early adulthood, body fat tends to increase, muscle mass tends to drop, and the reflexes begin to slow. The middle adult phase comes between 41 and 60. During this period, numerous medical problems often begin. Hearing and vision problems tend to set in, as do cardiovascular problems and diabetes. Vital signs are similar in early and middle adults. The leading cause of death for early adults (and until the age of 44) is unintentional injury.

From 45 to 60, however, cancer becomes the leading cause.

After 60, individuals are considered older adults. At this age, chronic medical issues are more likely to set in. Heart disease and COPD become more common. Vital signs will change, depending upon their health. Until 65, cancer is the leading cause of older adults. However, from 65 on, heart disease overtakes cancer as the leading cause. Typical life expectancy is 78 years, though it is estimated that maximum life expectancy is about 120 years old.

Part 5: Neurologic Emergencies

The brain is responsible for a wide variety of different functions, including breathing, movement, speech, sight, and swallowing. Different functions are controlled by different segments of the brain, such as the brainstem, cerebellum, and cerebrum. In addition, there are a series of nerves that conduct information between body and brain via electrical impulses. Emergency conditions related to the brain are known as neurologic emergencies. Though they tend to be more common in adults, they can potentially occur in children as well. Neurological conditions can range from mild to life threatening. They can present with a variety of different signs and symptoms, depending on the portion of the brain affected. Patient outcome for serious neurological emergencies depends upon quick recognition and prompt treatment.

One common indication of neurological conditions is a headache. In most cases, headaches are not a symptom of a serious condition; however, they can be a sign of some conditions such as a stroke or meningitis. The brain itself lacks pain receptors, so headaches tend to result from scalp, meninges, and surrounding blood vessels. Strokes, also called cardiovascular accidents or CVAs, are very serious medical emergencies, resulting from an interruption of the flow of blood to the brain and often caused by a clot. In medical terms, the inadequate flow of blood to an organ or part of the body is known as an ischemia. If this occurs in the brain, brain cells can die and permanent brain damage can occur. In the most serious cases of stroke, death can ensue.

Less serious strokes (mini-strokes) are called transient ischemic attacks, or TIAs. Though these are not life threatening and often do not often result in brain damage, they are indicators of more serious conditions and the patient should still be examined by a physician. Symptoms of a stroke include confusion, headache, facial droop and slurred speech. However, there are other conditions which can mimic these symptoms, such as hypoglycemia and the postictal state occurring after some seizures.

Treatment for strokes or TIAs include assessing ABC'S. Stroke patients often have trouble maintaining their airway. Begin oxygen therapy on any patient with hypoxia. Perform a neurological exam like the Cincinnati Prehospital Stroke Screen. This scale checks for facial droop, arm drift and slurred or normal speech. Determine the onset time of the symptoms. This information is critical for the receiving hospital. Check blood sugar since hypoglycemia can cause a patient to present with stroke symptoms. Transport as soon as possible. This is a very time sensitive emergency as some hospital treatments for strokes have a very short window of effectiveness.

Seizures are a result of a misfire of electrical activity. Patients will exhibit muscle rigidity and uncontrolled muscular activity, and may lose consciousness. If seizures last for longer than five minutes, or if they occur close enough together that the patient has no time to recover between them, the condition is known as status epilepticus. Most often, seizures are a product of epilepsy, the fourth most common neurological disorder. However, they may also result from traumatic brain injury, drugs, and brain tumors. If you encounter a seizure patient, one of the most important initial treatments is to maintain the airway.

Good BLS care is essential in treating seizure patients. Be sure the seizing patient is clear of dangerous objects and move them if necessary. Loosen restrictive clothing around the neck and airway. If a seizing patient cannot maintain their own airway use an appropriate airway adjunct. The best choice in this situation is a nasopharyngeal airway. (NPA) After securing the airway provide supplemental oxygen via non rebreather mask. If the patient's respirations are inadequate assist with a bag valve mask. If trauma is not suspected turn the patient onto their side (recover position) to allow fluids in the mouth to drain and keep the airway clear.

Another neurological condition commonly encountered is an altered level of consciousness, which is essentially the inability of the patient to think clearly. If the level of consciousness is profoundly altered, it is known as delirium, a condition characterized by incoherent speech and thought, illusions, and restlessness. This can result from a wide variety of conditions, such as brain infection, hyperglycemia, brain injury, drug and alcohol use, seizures, and strokes. When encountering a patient with an altered level of consciousness

(ALOC), it is important to determine and address the underlying cause, as different causes require different treatment.

Emergency response to neurological emergency follows the same pattern as with other emergencies. Scene size-up is the first step, allowing the responder to evaluate scene safety and issues which require an immediate response. Following the scene size-up, the responder should conduct a primary assessment, checking airway, breathing, and circulation for life threatening issues. Next, the patient's medical history should be taken. This can aid in the diagnosis of the problem and help to refine further treatment. The secondary survey then follows, providing a more complete, head-to-toe assessment of the patient's condition. It should be remembered that neurological conditions can change quickly, so the final step, ongoing reassessment during transport, is vital and should be attended with care.

Most neurological conditions require hospital attention, and emergency treatment is often limited to airway management and transport. When dealing with seizures, emergency treatment may include administering medicine to decrease seizure activity.

Part 6: Gastrointestinal and Urologic Emergencies

Since numerous organs take part in the function of the digestive and urological systems, these emergencies can arise in any one of them. These include the bladder, stomach, gallbladder, and intestine, and it is necessary to identify the problem before the proper treatment can be provided. A common symptom encountered by the EMT is acute abdomen, which is the sudden onset of abdominal pain. Potential causes include diverticulitis, gastroenteritis, and appendicitis, and the severity can range from mild to life threatening. Another common gastrointestinal condition is peritonitis, which is the inflammation of the peritoneum, the tissue that lines the abdominal cavity. A common cause is irritation caused by pus or blood. Also, due to the nature and function of the digestive and urological systems, perforations can leak waste materials into the body and cause serious complications.

Patient assessment in the event of a gastrointestinal emergency begins with scene size-up followed by a primary assessment. It should be remembered that in some cases, internal bleeding can ensue and low blood pressure or other life threatening symptoms may occur. After the primary assessment, take the medical history of the patient. Remember to ask about diarrhea and vomiting. In the secondary assessment, make sure to palpate the abdomen to check for tenderness. It is also important to monitor the patient carefully throughout reassessment, given the potential for gastrointestinal emergencies to cause shock and other serious conditions. Patients should be assessed for shock and treated promptly if they exhibit signs. Airway management is also crucial for vomiting patients, and care should be taken to avoid contamination.

Dialysis may be necessary in patients with kidney shut down or end stage renal disease. It is a procedure that substitutes for the function of the kidneys when they are not working sufficiently on their own. It also comes with potential side effects and presents unique medical emergencies, including infection vomiting, and bleeding at the access site. If dialysis medical emergencies are encountered in the field, responders should check airway, breathing, and circulation and provide prompt transport to the hospital.

Part 7: Endocrine and Hematologic Emergencies

The endocrine system uses chemical messengers called hormones to regulate body function. It includes a number of glands such as the adrenal glands, thyroid, and pancreas. If these glands secrete too little or too much of a hormone, endocrine emergencies result. A common endocrine dysfunction is diabetes, a condition resulting from the overproduction or underproduction of insulin. Insulin helps the body to process glucose into chemical energy. Diabetes can also result from the inability of the receptor cells to bind to the glucose molecule. In severe cases, diabetes can be life-threatening or cause severe disabilities.

Left unchecked, coma, kidney disease, and blindness can result.

One challenge of some forms of diabetes is hypoglycemia, which is a low level of glucose in the blood. Normal glucose levels are considered to be between 70-130. Anything below 70 is considered to be low. If hypoglycemia is identified, treatment can be offered promptly, potentially saving the patient's life. Symptoms include sweating tachycardia, confusion, blurred vision, and shakiness. Low blood sugar levels can also lead to acidosis, or the buildup of acid in the blood and tissues. If the level of glucose in the blood drops too low, altered levels of consciousness, unconsciousness, or seizures may result. It's important to diagnose the condition correctly, however, as altered levels of consciousness and seizures can result from a range of other conditions. Check blood sugar levels and take the patient's history prior to administering treatment.

Assessment, as always, begins with ensuring that the scene is safe. One potential hazard is the presence of needles, which may be present around diabetic patients for the injection of insulin. Move on to a primary assessment, remembering that diabetic emergency can interfere with breathing. Check the patient's blood sugar level with a glucometer. Also check the patient's level of consciousness, as this can indicate the severity of the emergency. Move on to the patient's medical history, noting the time of the last insulin injection and most recent meal. During transport, maintain ongoing assessment, as diabetic emergency can result in quick changes in status.

For hypoglycemic patients, treatment involves administering oral glucose. This can be administered in a gel, chewable tablet, or liquid. This is contraindicated only if the patient is unable to swallow. The most common form is gel, especially with patients showing an altered level of consciousness. In this case, the gel should be placed on a tongue depressor and placed between cheek and gum. Patients may also require airway management and treatment for shock. If patients are hyperglycemic, or experiencing an excess of blood sugar, then the initial treatment involves the administration of insulin.

Hematology is the study of the blood. A number of hematologic, or blood-related, emergencies can arise as well. These include thrombophilia, hemophilia, and sickle cell anemia. Each has its own symptoms and treatment. Patients with thrombophilia have blood that clots too easily, potentially blocking the flow of blood to vital organs. Hemophiliac patients have the opposite dysfunction, possessing blood that is unable to clot or clots too slowly. Even minor cuts can continue to bleed leading to excess blood loss. Internal bleeding is also a severe problem in these patients. Patients with sickle cell anemia have red blood cells that are compromised in terms of their ability to carry oxygen. These patients can become hypoxic and, in extreme cases, experience organ damage and pain crisis, recurrent episodes of pain occurring suddenly and often localized around the joints.

During the scene size-up, be alert for the presence of blood and take precautions to prevent contamination. Remember to use eye protection. Check the airway first, and evaluate the level of consciousness during the primary assessment. When taking history, find out about a history of hematologic conditions. Second assessment includes taking vitals. Remember that that patients experiencing sickle cell crisis will show a weak and rapid pulse. During transport, reassess frequently and monitor for changes in oxygen level and level of consciousness.

Part 8: Immunologic Emergencies

The immune system is composed of bone marrow, the spleen, lymph vessels, and lymph nodes. Lymph vessels and nodes trap bacteria in fluid where it can then be attacked and removed by lymphocytes. Bone marrow produces white and red blood cells, and the spleen helps to kill bacteria. The immune system is responsible for protecting the system from infection. However, it sometimes responds to otherwise harmless foreign particles, causing an allergic reaction. When the immune system is triggered, histamine, leukotrienes, and other chemicals are released.

In the presence of an allergen, the immune system overreacts and releases these chemicals in excess.

Symptoms of a mild allergic reaction include hives (also known as urticaria), sneezing, and watery eyes. Severe allergic reactions can block the airway, so checking airway and breathing is the first priority in affected patients. Another potential symptom is angioedema, which is stomach cramping alongside discolored patches or rashes on hands, feet, and arms, a swollen throat, and hoarseness. The most severe allergic reaction is known as anaphylaxis, or anaphylactic shock. Patients with severe allergies will often carry EpiPens, or single-use injectable doses of epinephrine, which can serve as immediate treatment in the event of exposure to the allergen.

Patients may be allergic to a range of different substances, including insect toxins, chemicals, plants, medications, and foods. Some people are allergic to penicillin, and it is critical for medical personnel to know this in order to avoid administering this or similar antibiotics to such a patient. A common chemical allergen is latex. Many people are allergic to the stings of wasps and bees. Common plant allergens include oak, ragweed, and pollen. A common fungal allergen is mold. Food allergies can also be quite severe, and some of the most common culprits are shellfish, peanuts, and milk.

As mentioned, the first step in handling patients with allergic reactions is to check the airway and breathing. When taking history, ask about known allergies. Taking vital signs, listening for breath sounds, and checking oxygen levels is critical in the secondary assessment. During reassessment, focus on airway management, monitoring respiration, and checking level of consciousness. Quick transport is also necessary. Aside from airway management and quick transport, emergency treatment for anaphylaxis typically involves the administration of epinephrine to improve blood flow, decrease airway swelling, and reduce bronchospasms. Auto-injectors with pre-measured doses of epinephrine are called

EpiPens and they are the usual method of administration for epinephrine.

Part 9: Pharmacology

Pharmacology is the branch of study related to medications, including their composition, preparation, action within the body, and methods of administration. Medications are used to treat and prevent illness and infection and to reduce pain. Each medication works differently, but they generally bind with receptor cells to either cause or block a particular effect within the body. The dose of a drug is proportional to the action it causes. In addition to the therapeutic effect, drugs also cause unwanted or unhelpful effects known as side effects.

Medications generally have two names: the brand name, and the generic name. Generic names are not capitalized, while brand names, those given by the manufacturer, are capitalized. Medication can also be classified as prescription, requiring a doctor's order, or over-the-counter, in which case it can be purchased without prescriptions. Medications can also be administered in a number of different ways. These include oral, such as swallowed pills or liquids, injections, which are placed under the skin into the muscle or bloodstream, respiratory, administered through inhalation, sublingual, or placed under the tongue, rectal, or administered through the rectum, or transcutaneous, or absorbed through the skin. Capsules, liquids, and tabs are oral medication. Injections or IVs can administer medications in a solution form. Metered dose inhalers and nebulizers are common ways to administer respiratory medications. Other forms include gases, patches, creams, lotions, and gels.

There are only a few medications which are within the scope of practice of EMTs. Many of these require contact with medical control to supervise the process. Common medications which EMTs administer are activated charcoal, nitroglycerin, epinephrine, aspirin, oral glucose, and supplemental oxygen. In addition, EMTs may assist a patient in the use of a metered dose inhaler. The administration of medications is a potential point of error and medication errors are potentially life threatening, so it's crucial to avoid mistakes.

To reduce the risk of error, follow the Six Rights of Medication Administration: right patient, right medication, right dose, right time, and right documentation. Medication errors include using the wrong route or administering the wrong dose. Both of these are examples of knowledge-based errors, which are providing the wrong medication, dose, or route of administration for the patient. The other form of medication error is administration-based, meaning that the EMT has provided a medication outside of their scope of practice. All errors should be documented and reported truthfully, and medical control should be informed immediately upon notice. It is also critical to provide all necessary care to prevent adverse reactions from the medication.

Part 10: Toxicology

The study of toxic substances is known as toxicology. It is common for emergency responders to be called to the scene to treat patients who have ingested or been exposed to a toxin or poison. The first step in treatment is to identify the problem. A number of the symptoms of poisoning occur in other illnesses as well, so thorough assessment is necessary. Toxins may come in the form of solids, liquids, or gases, and they can enter the body through inhalation, injection, absorption, or ingestion, though ingestion is the most common route.

There are a number of different poisons, including drugs and alcohol. Overdose on synthetic street drugs or opioids can result in cardiac arrest and a depression in respiratory function. Inhaled chemicals, like paint thinners and cleaning products, can cause cardiac complications. Food poison is commonly encountered. It results from the ingestion of salmonella, e. coli, or staphylococcus bacteria, among others, and shows symptoms of fever, diarrhea, stomach cramps, and vomiting. These symptoms present between two and twelve hours after ingestion.

Plants are another source of poisoning, especially in children, as several household plants are toxic. Mild symptoms include rashes, and more severe symptoms include life threatening circulatory and respiratory conditions. If a plant is the source of the poison, then the plant should be identified if at all possible, and the receiving hospital should be informed regarding about it for prompt and effective treatment. Severe poisoning from a variety of sources may cause hematemesis, which is the vomiting of blood. This results from bleeding in the upper gastrointestinal tract. If the poisoning is chemical in nature and the chemical is identified, then the material safety data sheet should contain information on what to do in the event of ingestion or exposure.

The primary treatments for most poisons are antidotes which neutralizes their effects. However, emergency response focuses on stabilizing the patient and transporting them quickly to the hospital. Begin by assessing the scene and taking all necessary safety precautions. Ensure that responding personnel are not exposed to toxic substances. Conduct a primary assessment of airway, breathing, and circulation. Take medical history, attempting to rule out other problems and pin down the time and nature of poisoning. In the second assessment, monitor vitals and check quickly for other symptoms. Ongoing assessment is then required to monitor changes in the patient's status and manage the airway. Remember that changes can occur abruptly in poisoned patients.

Part 11: Psychiatric Emergencies

There are a number of psychiatric emergencies which an EMT may encounter in the line of duty, from mental illnesses to behavioral or emotional crises. Mental illness like depression and bipolar disorder can affect mood, behavior, and thinking. Intense emotional reactions can cause emotional crisis, even in individuals without a mental illness. In both cases, an individual's capacity for normal functioning can be severely compromised. A behavioral crisis is similar to an emotional crisis in that it can occur in otherwise healthy individuals and interferes with normal function. In these instances, the patient may be uncooperative, agitated, and aggressive. They may display odd behavior and may become a threat to themselves or others. Psychiatric or behavioral emergencies may be organic or functional in nature. In organic psychiatric emergencies, the cause is physical, a disturbance of brain tissue. This disturbance is termed OBS or organic brain syndrome. Psychiatric emergencies are termed functional when no physical cause can be found.

One of the hazards in psychiatric emergencies is the potential unpredictability of the patient. It is vital to use a non-threatening approach that helps the patient to feel safe. Be direct, and begin by identifying yourself. Keep a safe distance. Use clear language and establish a calm atmosphere by being reassuring and honest. Avoid arguments or escalation.

One of the first steps is to determine whether or not you need law enforcement on scene. Explain all processes during the primary assessment to avoid making the patient more agitated. Taking history may be problematic, unless other people are present. Secondary assessment involves close observation, and reassessment should focus on monitoring status changes, noting especially if the patient becomes more agitated. If the patient is a danger to themselves or others, then restraints may be necessary. Make sure to be familiar with the protocol of your agency, and make safety the first priority. Mental incompetence also presents legal challenges, as treatment cannot be provided without consent. If this is the case, then it may be necessary for law enforcement to take the patient into protective custody and give consent on their behalf.

The psychological emergency may come in the form of acute psychosis. If this is the case, then the patient will tend to be out of touch with reality, hearing and seeing things that are not there. Acute psychosis may be brought on by extreme stress, drug use, or a mental illness like schizophrenia. Excited delirium is another potential psychological emergency. The patient experiencing this will exhibit impaired cognitive function, hallucination, and paranoia. This condition shows physical symptoms of dilated pupils, increased heart rate, and sweating. You may also encounter patients with PTSD, or post-traumatic stress disorder, a condition often developed after extremely stressful events. PTSD patients may be easily angered and unpredictable. Patients will exhibit fear, anxiety, and an exaggerated startle response. Remain calm and speak soothingly. Do not touch the patient without asking them, and explain all procedures prior to performing them.

Patients will sometimes be violent or suicidal. With violent patients, make sure to assess the risk of danger. Check into the history of the patient to see if there have been previous incidents of violence. Observe body language for aggression and tension. Listen carefully to language and tone, looking for signs of aggression like shouting. Assess the surroundings for weapons or things that can be used as weapons. Safety is paramount. Contact law enforcement if necessary. Patients undergoing an emotional crisis may be suicidal. Take any suicide threats seriously. Observe the patient carefully, looking out for signs of hopelessness, despair, or extreme sadness. Also watch for an inability to make eye contact and a complete lack of emotionality. Once again, be speak calmly and reassuringly, and bring in law enforcement to maintain the situation.

Part 12: Gynecological Emergencies

Gynecology is the field of study related to the female reproductive system. This includes inner structures such as the uterus, ovaries, and fallopian tubes, and outer structures such as the labia minora and labia majora. The vagina and cervix, which is the entry point from the vaginal into the cervix, are also included in this system. Another important area is the perineum, which, in gynecological terms, is the tissue between the anal and vaginal orifices.

This system is highly vascular and thus prone to injury. The ovaries produce eggs each month and send them into the fallopian tubes, where they await fertilization. This process is known as ovulation. After fertilization, the egg is implanted into the lining of the uterine wall. Issues with any of these structures are termed gynecological emergencies. Some common emergencies include infection or trauma. An EMT might encounter a patient with abnormal vaginal bleeding, sexually transmitted disease, or pelvic inflammatory disease, which typically occurs when sexually transmitted bacteria spread from the vagina to uterus, fallopian tubes, or ovaries. Another potential injury is laceration of the perineum.

During the scene size-up, one common hazard to keep in mind is the presence of blood, as bleeding can accompany a number of gynecological emergencies. Standard precautions apply to prevent exposure to the blood and potential contamination. Another important consideration should be kept in mind in the event of sexual assault. If a woman has been sexually assaulted, law enforcement should be brought on scene and a female EMT should attend to the patient if at all possible.

Check the patient for blood loss and resulting mental instability during the primary assessment. When taking history, look into the date of the patient's last menstrual period, known STDs, and the possibility of pregnancy. When dealing with a sexual assault the patient should be checked for additional injuries during the secondary assessment. Also check for abdominal tenderness and mental status and monitor vital signs. During reassessment, monitor blood pressure, especially if blood loss has occurred.

It is important to respect the patient's privacy as much as possible when responding to the emergency, as gynecological issues can be very sensitive and highly charged. Having a female work with the patient is best. Since bleeding can be an issue, monitor for signs of shock due to blood loss. Any lacerations should be treated with sterile dressings, and do not attempt to remove foreign objects. Remember that the female genitalia contain an abundance of nerve fibers, so injuries can be extremely painful.

Treatment will vary depending on the specific nature of the emergency. The main priorities are controlling any bleeding that might be present, assessing for injuries, and offering supportive care. Pain management is also a key consideration, as well as close monitoring during transport. Remember that the incident will be sensitive, and have a female EMT care for the patient if possible. In the event of sexual assault, it is important to bring law enforcement on the scene and follow all instructions for preserving evidence.

Part 13: Obstetrics and Neonatal Care

Medical emergencies often arise with pregnant women, women in labor, and those who have just given birth. Obstetrics is the practice of medicine dealing with pregnancy, and neonatal care is about dealing with babies in the first month of life. Any emergencies that occur are likely to impact both mother and child.

Building upon the anatomical information in the previous section, after the fertilized egg is implanted in the uterine wall, it becomes an embryo. The embryo continues to divide and develop in the uterus. The placenta develops as well, and it is linked to the developing fetus via the umbilical cord. The placenta supplies oxygen and nutrients to the fetus, and it is surrounded by fluid contained within an amniotic sac. This fluid provides cushioning and protection for the fetus.

The typical pregnancy lasts 40 weeks, though the child is considered fully developed (full-term) after 39 weeks of gestation, or fetal development. This time frame is broken into three equal periods, called trimesters. Term gestation means that a baby has been born at full-term, and is loosely considered to be between 37 and 42 weeks. Within a few weeks to a few hours before labor, the mother will experience lightening, which is a time when the baby settles into the pelvis. Many changes occur in the mother's body during this period due to the pregnancy hormones released during gestation. These include increased blood volume, slowed digestion, weight gain, and loose joints. During pregnancy, a number of different complications can occur. Some are minor, while others can be life-threatening to mother or child or both.

Common complications include pre-eclampsia, which is characterized by high blood pressure, protein in the urine, and sometimes damage to other organ systems like the kidneys or liver. Left untreated, it is potentially life threatening, so it should be addressed as quickly as possible.

Pregnant women may experience uterine bleeding, which is often a sign of problems with the uterus, though it can have other causes. One cause of uterine bleeding is abruptio placenta, which is a separation of the placenta from the uterine wall prior to childbirth. This is most common in the third trimester, but can happen at any time during pregnancy. It is also possible to develop diabetes during pregnancy, known as gestational diabetes.

Another potential complication in pregnancy is trauma. An injury may cause excess bleeding, due to the mother's increased volume of blood. The abdomen is an especially vulnerable area, and if trauma has been sustained here, then abdominal pain and vaginal bleeding commonly occur. This is important to remember in the event of car accidents, as seat belts can cause abdominal trauma in pregnant women if worn improperly.

It's important to remember that there are different cultural perspectives regarding pregnancy and how it should be handled. Some cultures prohibit males from treating pregnant women. Their cultural values should be respected if possible by having a female responder treat the patient. There are special considerations with regard to age as well. Low birth weight is more prevalent in pregnant teens, and it is also possible that the teen is unaware that they are pregnant. It is best to have the parent present and to understand your state laws regarding the care of pregnant teens. Some states afford adult rights to pregnant teens in the medical care they receive.

The first thing to keep in mind when arriving on scene is to avoid overlooking standard precautions in the face of urgency. The emotions will be high with labor or pregnancy complications, and both the mother and family members are likely to be extremely anxious. However, do a proper scene size up and then move into the primary assessment. Check airway, breathing, and circulation, and determine whether the patient is in labor. Watch for bleeding or problems with breathing. When taking history, find out how far the patient is along in their pregnancy and ask about previous complications. Secondary assessment should include vitals and a check for fetal movement. Watch for hypotension, as this may be an indication of bleeding. During reassessment, monitor vitals and watch for changes in the patient's status.

Normal delivery, or labor, has three stages. First, the cervix dilates. When the child begins to crown, its head will be visible through the vaginal opening. This signals the end of the first stage of labor and the beginning of the second: delivery of the child. Once the child has been delivered completely, the second stage ends. The final stage is the delivery of the placenta, ending when it has been fully delivered. If you encounter a patient in the early stages of labor, the proper treatment will be to monitor the patient and provide quick transport.

If labor is far enough along, it may be necessary to deliver the child on scene or even in the ambulance. If so, the first step is to make sure your OB kit is on hand and place the woman in delivery position. The woman should then focus on breathing and pushing in time with the contractions. As the head emerges, it should be supported. If the cord is around the neck, it should be gently lifted over the head. Do not force it. The child will then rotate to one side to clear the shoulders through the birth canal. As soon as the baby's head appears suction the mouth and nose with a bulb syringe. After the shoulders have emerged, the rest of the body should come through relatively easily.

The child should be dried immediately upon delivery and warmly wrapped with blankets. Hypothermia is a major concern for newborns. Then, if necessary, the nose and then the mouth should be suctioned. Often, the child's first feces, called meconium, is passed in the womb. It may block the airway and should be suctioned out if necessary. One minute after birth, and again at the five minute mark, the APGAR score should be tested. This is an assessment of the child's appearance, pulse, grimace response or reflexes, activity, and respiration. For appearance if the baby is completely pink they get 2 points. If their body is pink but their extremities are blue they receive 1 point. If they are blue or pale they receive 0 points. For Pulse, if they have a heart rate over 100 beats per minute they get 2 points. If their heart rate is below 100 beats per minute they score 1. If they have no pulse the score is 0. For grimace they get 2 points for active motion. This includes sneezing, coughing or pulling away. If the baby has some flexion of the extremities they score 1 point. If they are flaccid they score 0 points. For activity if the baby is actively moving they score 2 points. If they are only moving their arms and legs they score 1 point. If they are not moving they score 0 points. And lastly for respiration if they have a vigorous cry they score 2 points. For slow or irregular respiration they score 1. If breathing is absent they score 0. Apgar scores of 7 or greater are considered good to excellent, while scores of 3 or less are considered poor. If the child is not crying, first stimulate them by flicking the soles of the feet. If no reaction ensues, then administer resuscitation with chest compressions and manual ventilation. Next, place the infant on the mother's chest to facilitate bonding with skin to skin contact.

Wrap the child in a clean, dry blanket to keep it warm.

After the cord stops pulsating, it should be clamped and cut. Place the clamp approximately 8-10 inches from the baby. Place a second clamp approximately 2 inches from the first, then cut the cord between the clamps. Never cut the cord of a baby who is not breathing unless the cord is around the baby's neck. Normal vital signs for a newborn are 120-160 heart beats per minute and 40-60 breaths per minute.

Watch for significant bleeding (more than 500mL) prior to the delivery of the placenta or for bleeding that continues for a significant time afterwards. If bleeding occurs, absorb blood with a sterile pad, administer oxygen, and transport the patient to the hospital promptly. The placenta should be delivered shortly after the delivery of the child and with little assistance. This should take place within a few minutes after the child has been delivered. If delivery of the placenta does not occur within this time frame, the patient should be transported to the hospital and transferred into care of receiving personnel as quickly as possible without undue risk.

Many of the complications in delivery arise due to the positioning of the child in the womb. In normal deliveries, the head is oriented downward and is the first part of the child to pass through the birth canal. If the feet or butt of the child is leading, then it is known as a breech delivery. This is a complicated delivery, requiring more effort and assistance and risking trauma to the child. When the umbilical cord prolapses, then it comes out prior to the head. In a limb presentation birth, an arm or leg is delivered first. Limb presentation births cannot be done in the field, so the emergency treatment is to monitor the patient and transport her promptly to the hospital. Upon encountering any birth complications, it will be necessary to call ACLS, Advanced Cardiovascular Life Support, for guidance and assistance.

Part 14: Pediatric Emergencies

Though medical emergencies are largely the same in adults and children, there are some emotional and physical differences that are necessary to understand to effectively treat pediatric patients. In most instances, when working with pediatric patients, you must also deal with parents or caregivers. Show respect and make sure they are fully informed throughout the process. Often, the caregivers and parents will need emotional support to counter their fear and helplessness. Depending on the age of the child, it may be necessary to communicate with them as well, clearly, honestly, and in a non-threatening way. The airways of children are smaller than those of adults and their tongue is larger proportionately. This makes intubation more difficult. The child's heart rate is faster than that of an adult. Their bones tend to be softer and more prone to fracture, and the abdominal muscles have not developed as much, meaning that their abdomens are more prone to trauma.

To treat a pediatric patient effectively, it is important to understand developmental stages.

Infants may tend to cry and will rarely remain still for treatment or assessment. When dealing with toddlers, they may experience separation anxiety if separated from their parents, so it will be helpful to keep them close during assessment and treatment. When children come to preschool age, their language capacities have developed enough to respond to simple questions about their symptoms and where they feel pain. Children of this age should be permitted to make simple choices if possible, such as whether they would like their blood pressure measured with the right or left arm.

Pediatric assessment begins with making sure that you have the appropriate equipment to treat a child. Upon arrival, size up the scene quickly to identify aspects of the environment which may have contributed to the medical emergency. Primary assessment focuses on airway, breathing and circulation, just as with adults. Also use the pediatric assessment triangle (PAT) to do a 30-second evaluation of muscle tone, work of breathing, and level of consciousness. Listen for grunting at the end of the exhalation, as this can indicate extra work devoted to breathing. The caregivers or parents will need to be relied upon for medical history, as the child will often be unable to provide the information accurately and comprehensively. Close monitoring during reassessment is also necessary to catch any status changes as they occur.

Common pediatric respiratory emergencies can be acute conditions, chronic conditions, or infections. Acute conditions involve airway obstruction due to choking. Infections can include pneumonia, pertussis, RSV, croup, and epiglottitis. One example of a chronic condition is asthma. The smaller airway of children makes them more prone to the quick development of breathing problems. Look for nasal flaring, wheezing, grunting, retractions, level of distress, and work of breathing to identify respiratory emergencies. Treatment often requires supplemental oxygen to prevent hypoxia. In severe cases, respiratory arrest can lead to circulatory emergencies. In fact, this is the most common cause of circulatory emergency in children. Respiratory failure leads to a drop in oxygen levels, which then develops into bradycardia and later cardiac arrest. Treatment and ACLS protocols are the same as in adults, but medication doses are lowered.

If pediatric patients experience neurological emergencies, the most common causes are hypoxia, seizure, or hypoglycemia. Check for an altered level of consciousness, which often presents in children as combativeness, irritability, or sleepiness. Gastrointestinal complaints like stomach pain are most often of little concern, but there are some more serious causes. There is the potential for injury or infection. Appendicitis is another potential cause, and it is among the most common gastrointestinal emergencies likely to be encountered in children. Symptoms include fever, abdominal pain, and vomiting. The abdomen will be tender when palpated. Fevers are another common issue in pediatric patients, often resulting from infection. Other causes include gastroenteritis and pneumonia. High fevers can also cause febrile seizures. These are most common in toddlers and infants. They are usually not serious and treatment is rarely necessary, but the patient may require airway management during transport.

Poisoning is often encountered in the field with pediatric patients, as children are more likely to ingest things in their surroundings. Some of the sources can include alcohol, cleaning products and vitamins. Signs include an altered level of consciousness, vomiting, and sleepiness. Treatment varies depending on the poison, so try to determine the substance responsible for the poisoning, when it occurred, and how much was ingested. Also check to see if choking has resulted. The poison control hotline can provide information as to proper treatment for the specific poison. Activated charcoal is often administered for emergency treatment.

Trauma in children can result from a variety of sources, including sport injuries, falls, and motor vehicle accidents. If the child's language development is insufficient, they may be unable to tell you where they hurt, meaning that you will have to use witness reports and exams to determine the extent, and sometimes the nature, of the injury. Treatment varies depending on the injury. The lower blood volume of children also makes them more prone to shock if they have lost blood or are bleeding internally. Monitor for shock and treat when necessary.

Drowning is another common challenge. In fact, it is the second leading cause of death in patients between one and four years of age. The time of submersion will influence the severity of the symptoms. Mild symptoms include choking and coughing. Serious symptoms include cardiac arrest and apnea, and will require resuscitation. Treatment includes advanced cardiac life support, management of airway, breathing and circulation, and prompt transport.

In the event of a disaster involving multiple pediatric patients less than eight years old, jumpSTART triage may be necessary. This categorizes patients based on their ability to breathe, respond to painful stimuli, and walk.

Tags are assigned to indicate severity: red for serious, yellow for second priority, and green for minor problems. Treatment is prioritized on the basis of severity.

Emergency medical responders are legally obligated to report suspicions of child abuse or neglect. You may encounter these children in the field. Look for multiple injuries at different stages of healing, unexplained decreased levels of consciousness, and marks that could be caused by cigarette burns. Infants are susceptible to shaken baby syndrome, which can cause severe brain damage. Early signs include vomiting, bluish skin, shakes or tremors, breathing issues, and signs of drowsiness, peaking from four to six hours after the event. Neglected children may appear malnourished, uncared for, and dirty. Remember that it is suspicion that must be reported, not proof. Prioritize the needs of the child and err on the side of caution.

Every year, 3500 babies dies every year in the United States alone from sudden infant death syndrome (SIDS). This is the unexplained death of an infant. It is more common in infants born with a low birth weight and those with mothers that smoked during pregnancy. Rates were higher prior to the campaign encouraging mothers to put their babies to sleep on their backs, but it still happens frequently enough that it is not uncommon to encounter it in the field. Another condition is the ALTE, or apparent life threatening event. The child will be unresponsive and apneic, but breathing resumes. When encountering SIDS or ALTE cases in the field, check the environment for objects in the crib or signs of abuse.

Part 15: Geriatric Emergencies
There are unique considerations to keep in mind when dealing with geriatric patients, those 65 years old and older. Many of the medical issues will be similar to those of younger adults, but each geriatric patient will have specific considerations. One common issue is the tendency for older adults to be living on fixed incomes, which can cause them to skip medications in order to save money. Problems with memory and hearing may be present in many geriatric patients. Make sure

to speak slowly, use eye contact, and communicate clearly. Give the patient enough time to respond to your questions. Have respect and explain all procedures clearly and completely before performing them. It is more common for older patients to suffer from complications to common illnesses. Finally, the leading causes of death for geriatric patients include cancer, stroke, and heart disease.

There are a number of changes that happen as we age, though the process is both gradual and individual. Lifestyle and self-care have an impact on the speed of decline, though bones, heart, and lungs will all tend to deteriorate over time. The lung tissue will tend to lose elasticity, and the breathing muscles lose tone, impacting the ease of breath. Finally, older patients may tend to become more inactive. Taken together, this makes the geriatric patient more susceptible to pneumonia and pulmonary embolism.

The arteries will also tend to thicken, raising blood pressure and increasing the likelihood of heart disease. As the situation progresses, it could manifest as heart failure, stroke, or heart attack. In the short run, the patient may experience syncope or other symptoms of circulatory emergency. Changes in the nervous system include decreases in smell, vision, and hearing. Cognitive issues may arise as well, with memory problems being the most common and earliest symptoms. Other potential manifestations of neurological decline include a loss of balance and dementia or delirium.

Alongside these changes, the gastrointestinal system will tend to decline as well. This can lead to a reduction in saliva and gastric fluids, which in turn lead to a higher risk of aspiration. Other potential complications include constipation, diverticulitis, and ulcers. Changes in the renal system include lowered kidney function and urinary incontinence, urinary problems due to an enlarged prostate, and bladder infections.

Endocrine issues include challenges regulating body temperature and compromised metabolism. Hormone production lowers, interfering with the coordination of other bodily functions. One of the most common and challenging results of this is diabetes. Finally, the immune system tends to be less effective in geriatric patients, making them more susceptible to disease and infection. Symptoms and signs of infection may include altered mental status, fever, weight loss, and falls. The compromised immune system of geriatric patients also makes them more prone to serious illnesses like MRSA and VRE, so you should familiarize yourself with these conditions before working with geriatric patients exhibiting these symptoms.

It is common for older patients to be on a wide range of medications or polypharmacy. In addition, the geriatric patient may not metabolize medications in the same way as younger adults. The decline in gastrointestinal and kidney function may increase the amount of time that medication remains in the body before it is metabolized or excreted. The implication of these factors is that geriatric patients are at risk of drug interactions or taking too much medication. Patient history is critical to correctly identify and treat complications resulting from medication error.

Some geriatric patients are at risk for behavioral or emotional crises. They may be experiencing depression, a loss of purpose, or a lack of fulfillment. Severe crises may include suicide attempts. Take suicide threats seriously and treat these patients with respect, addressing them calmly and with compassion and sincerity.

One mnemonic for the assessment of geriatric patients is GEMS: geriatric, environment, medical conditions, and social assessment. Their environment will give clues about their condition. An understanding of medical history and medications is critical for proper treatment and to understand the physical and mental condition of the patient. Social assessment is equally important, as social context offers fulfillment and purpose. This also addresses the degree to which the patient can perform daily living skills and care for themselves.

In all cases, assessment begins with scene safety. Many geriatric patients live alone, and their homes may become cluttered. This can interfere with treatment and potentially create unsafe conditions. If this is observed, then they may require more assistance in daily living. Primary assessment follows the normal protocol, emphasizing levels of consciousness. This may be compromised due to illness or infection. Medical history is important, as geriatric patients are more likely to be on medications or have a history of medical incidents which could help to evaluate the current issue or have a bearing on the course of treatment. Vitals are key in the secondary assessment though it should be remembered that they differ somewhat in older patients than younger ones. During reassessment, watch for changes in status and any signs of instability which require treatment.

Osteoporosis is a loss of bone density, and it tends to be a progressive condition in older patients. This means that they are more likely to experience fractures. Changes in the muscle tissues, circulatory system, and skin raise the risk of other injuries as well. Pelvic and hip fractures are common, and complications are likely in geriatric patients. Falls are a common source of fractures and traumatic injury, and they are more likely given the tendency for the sense of balance to decline. It is important to assess the reason for the fall, though it may be difficult to pinpoint the exact reason. Try to determine whether environmental factors or medical conditions caused the fall, as this will help to provide effective treatment.

Many patients will be in geriatric care facilities such as nursing homes or assisted living facilities. These facilities offer varied levels of care ranging from skilled nursing care to medication and daily living skills. If called to treat a patient at one of these facilities, the staff can be helpful in taking medical history and providing information on the patient's daily conditions. Unfortunately, there are some instances in which elders are neglected or abused, in these facilities or by caregivers at home. Signs of elder abuse include self-destructive behavior, repeated soft-tissue injuries, overly defensive answers about these injuries, and chronic pain with a cause. Other physical signs include decubitus ulcers (bedsores), multiple injuries in various states of healing, burns, and pressure bruising. Just as with child abuse, EMTs are legally obligated to report suspicions of abuse or neglect as per the policy of their agency.

At some point, we all face death. In geriatric patients, this challenging reality looms ever closer. And, in the field of medicine, you will encounter it at some point. Some geriatric patients have put in place do not resuscitate orders (DNRs) or advance directives, orders which outline the patient's desires for health care and their wishes for friends and families. It is important to verify DNRs before limiting or discontinuing resuscitation efforts, but it is equally important to respect the wishes of these patients after they have been confirmed. Dealing with death and dying can be challenging, not only for the patient, but also for the family and loved ones. It's necessary to show respect and compassion, along with gentleness and sincerity, when encountering these patients and their families.

Section 5: Trauma

As mentioned before, there are two kinds of calls that an EMT will face in the field: medical emergencies and trauma. Until this point, we have focused on medical emergencies. Now, it is time to turn our attention to trauma. Trauma is defined as a physical or emotional injury. Physical trauma is damage to any part of the body. It can result from an act of violence or an accident, and it is the leading cause of death in people under 40. The human body is both extremely resilient and extremely fragile. With proper treatment, it can recover from damage to almost any part of the body. Without this treatment, even small injuries can have serious complications.

Emotional trauma is the result of an extremely stressful situation. Just like the body, the mind is capable of withstanding extremely stressful events like natural disaster, multi-casualty incidents, or rape. However, if this stress is not dealt with in healthy ways, it can result in shock, denial, and more long-term complications like PTSD. While the EMT will encounter both of these kinds of trauma in the field, this section is devoted to different types of physical trauma, their signs and symptoms, and emergency treatment.

Part 1: Trauma Basics

At the very core, there is an element of physics involved with physical trauma. Traumatic injuries occur when the body's tissues are exposed to energy levels beyond their tolerance. The mechanism of injury (MOI) is the specific forces or energy transmission that has been applied to the body and has resulted in injury. A complete understanding of this requires a review of Newton's Three Laws of Motion. 1. Inertia: an object in motion will stay in motion, and an object at rest will stay at rest, unless acted upon by an outside force. 2. Force: The amount of force delivered is a product of mass and acceleration. 3. For every action, there is an equal and opposite reaction.

Aside from thermal energy, which causes burns, there are three types of energy related to trauma: kinetic energy, potential energy, and work energy. Kinetic energy is the energy of motion. Work energy is force times distance. Potential energy is mostly associated with falls or falling objects. It is the energy stored in a body due to gravity, weight, and height above the ground. When an object falls, its potential energy is transformed into kinetic energy. Kinetic energy doubles when the mass doubles, but quadruples when the speed doubles. When kinetic energy is suddenly stopped, as in the case of impact, it transforms into work energy. If the energy is in excess of what the tissue can handle, the result is trauma.

The mechanism of injury is the where, what, how, and when of the energy absorbed into the tissues. It is how the trauma occurs and what part of the body it is absorbed into. The mechanism of injury itself can be considered significant or non-significant. A non-significant mechanism of injury is not considered to have a high likelihood of resulting in a life-threatening injury, while a significant mechanism is considered to have a high likelihood of it. During primary assessment of trauma patients, the index of suspicion is the likelihood of a specific injury. High index of suspicion should be maintained for patients in motor vehicle crashes with significant damage to the vehicle, those that have suffered a fall from a significant height and hose that have sustained penetrating damage.

Trauma can be described as either penetrating or blunt force. Blunt force trauma does not cause the skin to break. It is non-invasive, but may cause internal injuries including internal bleeding and organ damage. Signs can include redness, swelling, bruising, tenderness, and abrasions. One case in which blunt force trauma is common is in a motor vehicle collision. Each collision is a forced deceleration as a moving object hits a stationary object. Each motor vehicle collision is actually three collisions: 1. The collision between the vehicle and another vehicle or outside object, 2. Collision between driver or passenger and the interior of the vehicle, and 3. The collision between the internal organs and the outer wall of the body. One particular mechanism of injury for blunt force trauma is related to head collisions and the resulting trauma to the brain tissue. The coup brain injury is trauma absorbed by the portion of the brain receiving the blow. The contrecoup brain injury occurs when the moving head strikes a stationary object. It is an injury which occurs on the opposite side of the head.

Injuries may also result from penetrating trauma, which is force that penetrates the skin and enters into the portion of the body beneath point of entry. This results in both internal and external wounds. When dealing with projectiles, the velocity of the projectile is more important than the mass, as this is what carries the bulk of the kinetic energy. The trajectory of the projectile determines its passage through the body. The first step in dealing with penetrating injury is to slow the bleeding. Next, when dealing with a projectile, check for exit wounds to determine whether or not the bullet has left the body, and to slow bleeding from the exit wound if necessary. It should also be remembered that a patient will often experience cavitation with a bullet wound. Temporary cavitation is a pressure wave which spreads out from the path of the bullet and can produce distant damage. After the pressure wave has passed, position of the tissue recovers. Secondary cavitation results from gaps in the tissue which remain after the tissue has recovered from primary cavitation.

Trauma resulting from explosive blasts falls into four categories: primary, secondary, tertiary, and quaternary. Primary injuries are a result of the initial pressure wave. These can rupture the ear drum or create pulmonary blast injuries, ruptures of the lung tissue. Secondary injuries are caused by projectiles driven with force away from the site of the explosion. Tertiary injuries result from the blast of wind released by the explosion. This can throw the body away from the blast point and into solid objects, potentially causing fractures, traumatic amputations, and brain injury. Finally, quaternary injuries cover burns and anything else not covered by the other three categories. The force of an explosion can also force air into injured veins or arteries, causing an arterial air embolism.

When an injury or injuries affect more than a single bodily system, it causes multisystem trauma. Multisystem trauma is handled as if it is life threatening, as the injuries may be extremely acute and require prompt intervention from medical personnel with a wide range of different disciplines. When encountering a trauma patient, one of the most important things to remember is the golden hour, also known as the golden period or golden time. This is the period immediately following a traumatic event in which prompt medical intervention is most likely to prevent death. When responding to trauma patients, combine patient assessment with vital signs, visual clues, signs and symptoms, and the chief complaint of the patient. Given the need for prompt response, the assessment must be done quickly and thoroughly and in a timely fashion.

There are fourteen Golden Principles for Pre-Hospital Trauma Care. These principles serve as a guideline for emergency response to trauma patients. Principle one is to ensure safety of the patient and responders. This involves anticipating hazards and including all necessary precautions, such as law enforcement for violent crimes and personal protective equipment to prevent contamination. The second principle is scene assessment to determine if additional resources are necessary. Third is to determine the kinematics and mechanism of the injury. The fourth principle is to perform a patient assessment for life-threatening conditions. Check airway, breathing and circulation, and look into level of consciousness. If the patient is bleeding heavily, this should be addressed prior to the ABC's. It should also be remembered that geriatric patients, pregnant women, and children may be experiencing more serious conditions than it appears. They may also experience systemic influences and may decompensate rapidly.

The fifth principle is to maintain the airway and stabilize the cervical spine. Use of nasopharyngeal or oropharyngeal airways may be used for ventilation and endotracheal intubation may be required if necessary. If these airways are inaccessible, then cricothyroidotomy may be performed. Capnometry may also be used to monitor carbon dioxide levels. Intubation is indicated for patients with altered mental status that affects tongue position, airway or pulmonary burns, ventilation required due to decreased minute volume or decreased ventilation rate, the requirement of high supplemental oxygen to maintain blood oxygen levels of 95% or more, or a Glasgow Coma Score of 8 or less. This leads to the sixth principle, which is to provide supplemental oxygen if the patient requires it to maintain at least 95% dissolved oxygen in the blood.

The seventh principle is to control significant eternal hemorrhaging or bleeding. This may require direct pressure to the bleeding site with pressure dressing, a gloved hand and or elastic bandages. Elevating the extremity is also a method of bleeding control and should be done secondary and in conjunction with direct pressure. Elevate the limb above the heart. Consider laying the patient down to help facilitate elevation of the extremity. It may also require a single or double tourniquet if the pressure bandages are insufficient. Check local protocols for tourniquet use. Pressure points may also be utilized in the upper and lower extremities if bleeding does not stop and and continues to soak through the dressings. Finally, pressure pads impregnated with hemostatic agents may be packaged into the wound with pressure applied for three minutes. It should be remembered that resuscitation will not be successful if there is ongoing external hemorrhaging. The eighth golden principle is to provide basic shock therapy. This includes an assessment of the patient's whole body to look for additional injuries. The patient should also be covered to prevent hypothermia. Splints should be provided in the event of musculoskeletal injury. In all breaks except for a mid-shaft fracture of the femur, this can be done by splinting the patient to a backboard. For the femur, a traction splint will be necessary.

The ninth principle is spinal immobilization, if indicated. Indications for spinal immobilization in the event of a blunt trauma include alcohol or drug intoxication, an inability of the patient to communicate, altered levels of consciousness, anatomic abnormalities, spinal tenderness, neurologic complaints, neck pain, or sensory or motor deficits. For penetrating trauma, indications include motor or sensory deficits or spine-related neurologic complaints. The tenth principle is that critically injured patients should be transported to the nearest appropriate trauma facility. It is important to remember that emergency responders cannot treat internal hemorrhage or provide blood to replace the loss of red blood cells and the oxygen they carry. In both instances, the responder should spend as little time on scene as possible and should be familiar with the different levels of trauma care and the hospitals in their area which provide it.

Principle eleven is to provide IV fluid replacement during transport or while awaiting extrication. The twelfth principle is that the patient's history should be taken and the secondary assessment initiated only once all life-threatening conditions should be assessed. The thirteenth principle is to provide pain relief if possible and unless contraindicated. Finally, the responder should provide the receiving facility accurate and ongoing communication regarding the patient's status. This includes the pre-arrival warning, the verbal report when transferring the patient, and the written PCR covering the condition, kinematics, assessment results, the interventions administered, and the response to these interventions.

In order to perform effective assessment, the responder should be aware of the RTS, the Revised Trauma Score, which is based on the systolic pressure, the GCS, or Glasgow Coma Scale, and the patient's respiratory rate. The GCS describes the level of consciousness in patients with traumatic brain injury. As a final note, it is important for the responder to be familiar with the key aspects of assessment for different forms and regions of trauma. With critical injuries, scene time should be made as short as possible, which means that responders should be familiar with the different forms of transportation available, as well as the classification system of different trauma centers. A key concept is the platinum 10, the first ten minutes after the arrival of the responder on the scene. The overall goal of the emergency medical service in responding to trauma is to provide the safest, highest quality of care in pre-hospital treatment, and to provide prompt transport to the appropriate receiving center.

As trauma can affect any part of the body and involve multiple organ systems, the responder must have a strong grasp of the cardiovascular system, including both anatomy and physiology. This includes an understanding of perfusion, which is the pumping of blood through organs and tissues. It is also important to understand the impact of inadequate perfusion on critical systems. External bleeding can result in a loss of blood volume, which impacts the ability of the body to provide adequate perfusion. If too much blood is lost, the body will go into hypovolemic shock as the body is unable to supply adequate perfusion to critical organs and tissues. With critical external hemorrhaging, the first step is to stop blood loss. Hemophilia is also an important condition to understand, as it prevents blood from clotting without intervention. In hemophiliac patients, it is even more crucial to reduce blood flow as soon and as much as possible. Bleeding from the nose, ears, and mouth can be a sign of very serious conditions, including skull injury, esophageal disease, clotting disorders, or facial trauma. Alternately, it can indicate upper respiratory infection, digital trauma, or hypertension.

Internal bleeding is also life-threatening, and in the event of suspected internal bleeding, the patient should be transported to the appropriate trauma care facility without delay. Signs include pain at the site of injury, nausea and vomiting, sweaty, pale, and clammy skin, a swollen, tight abdomen, breathlessness, extreme thirst, and finally, a lack of consciousness. Additional signs include dark tarry stools or those with bright red blood, the presence of bright red blood or blood the color of dark coffee grounds in the vomit, or bleeding from an orifice.

If the patient enters hemorrhagic shock, they will show signs of weakness and dizziness, anxiety, restlessness or combativeness, an altered mental state, a pale, thready pulse, dropping blood pressure, delayed capillary refill, and dilated pupils that respond sluggishly. Detection of internal bleeding is more challenging, and it cannot be effectively treated in the field, so prompt hospital transport is crucial. The responder should review all steps for the assessment of patients both for internal and external bleeding, and ensure that they are fully familiarized with signs, symptoms, and methods for stopping the flow of blood in external hemorrhages, and preventing further injury with internal bleeding. This should include the use of pelvic binders and the proper treatment for open-book pelvic fractures.

Part 2: Soft Tissue Injuries

Soft tissue injuries are those sustained to the skin and the layers directly beneath it. The skin is integral for a number of different functions, including retaining water, regulating temperature, forming a pathway for the nerves, and providing a protective layer against pathogens. The soft tissue itself is composed of layers. The epidermis is the outermost portion, creating an outer waterproof barrier. Beneath this are the dermis, which contains hair follicles and sweat glands, as well as connective tissue, and the hypodermis, which is made of fat and connective tissue. Beneath this is a layer of fascia which surrounds all of the muscles. Also included in the soft tissue are the mucous membranes, which line the body cavities such as the gut and tubular organs.

Injuries to the soft tissue come in three forms: open, closed, and burns. In closed soft tissue injuries, the skin is not broken, but the tissue is damaged beneath. Open soft-tissue injuries are those in which the skin or mucous membrane has been broken. This brings about the possibility of pathogens. Burns result from an excess of energy transferred into the site of the trauma. Burns may come in the form of thermal energy, electricity, chemicals, or radiation.

Closed soft-tissue injuries result from blunt-force trauma. Signs and symptoms include discoloration, swelling, and pain at the site of the injury. Some common signs of closed soft tissue injuries are ecchymosis, contusions, crushing injuries, and hematomas. Ecchymosis is the discoloration of the skin from bleeding beneath, typically caused by bruising. Contusions are bruises, or regions of discoloration and swelling of the soft tissue in which blood vessels have been ruptured. Hematomas are discoloration and lumps caused by blood swelling beneath the site of the trauma, contusions.

Crushing injuries occur when the body is compressed by an object or between two heavy objects. If the crushing force is too strong, then it can cause crushing injury to a skeletal muscle. A common result of this is crush syndrome, which is shock or renal failure after the skeletal muscle has been crushed. Compartment syndrome is another common result of crush injury. Compartment syndrome is where the crushing of a portion of the body restricts blood flow to the tissues beyond. Signs of either crushing injury or compartment syndrome include the "Five Ps". These are pain, pallor, paresthesia, which is a burning or tingling sensation in the hands, feet, and limbs, poikilothermia, which is a coolness to the skin, and pulselessness in the affected region. Treatment includes supplemental oxygen and intravenous fluid. In extremely severe cases, amputation may be necessary to prevent necrosis and infection from spreading.

When a patient suffers an open soft tissue injury, the skin is broken, meaning that there is the potential for contamination. These injuries can come in a variety of different forms. Abrasions or avulsions occur when the soft tissue is scraped or gashed. Abrasions are superficial, or no deeper than the epidermis, while avulsions are scrapes which remove all layers of the skin and result in a loose flap of skin. Abrasions are treated by cleaning the wound with soap and water as well as an antiseptic wash. Antibiotic ointment is then administered, and the wound is dressed with a dry dressing. Avulsions require sterile irrigation, followed by replacing the flap and dressing the wound, so long as the tissue is not completely torn away.

Open soft tissue injuries may also come in the form of lacerations, or irregular tears, incisions, or cuts from sharp-edged objects, and penetration wounds resulting from impaled objects. Open soft-tissue injuries are easier to diagnose, as the trauma is visible. However, they require treatment for potential contamination and for bleeding. The potential for contamination makes open soft tissue wounds difficult to triage. Assessment of both open and closed tissue injuries includes sizing up the scene, determining mechanism of injury, performing primary assessment and immediate treatment, and then performing secondary assessment and reassessment. The potential for hypovolemic shock and other life-threatening conditions should be assessed in the case of severe closed soft tissue injuries.

Immediate assessment and triage is necessary in all soft tissue injuries. Critical closed soft tissue wounds include compound fractures. The mnemonic for the treatment of closed soft tissue wounds is RICES: rest, ice, compression, elevation, and splinting. For open soft tissue wounds, bites, closed fractures neck injuries, impaled objects, and abdominal injuries are considered significant and requiring careful and prompt attention. Impaled objects should not be removed, as this could cause the bleeding to intensify. Pressure should be placed to either side of the object. Evisceration is a particularly serious form of abdominal open wound in which the organs are exposed. Treatments for evisceration will include the use of an occlusive dressing. The responder should be familiar with all key treatment skills for severe open and closed soft tissue injuries.

Burns are the third form of soft tissue injury. Potential results include circulatory complications such as challenges to cardiac output, impact to blood volume, and edema. Plasma can be leaked in and around the tissue due to an increase in capillary permeability. Since the skin has been breached, there is the possibility of infection, pain, and dehydration. Other potential complications include neurovascular compromise, shock, irregular body temperature, and compartment syndrome. Burns to the face can cause airway compromise, while those which surround an entire portion of the body, circumferential burns, can produce swelling which cuts off circulation.

Burns are classified by degree according to their severity, including the depth and extent of the burn and the areas of the body involved. First degree burns are superficial, resulting in tenderness, red skin, and pain. Second degree burns have partially extended through the epithelium. They produce blisters, red or white mottled skin with is moist to the touch and mottled. Third degree burns extend through the full thickness of the epithelium. They result in a leathery appearance, charring, dark brown or white skin which is hard to the touch. The nerves are destroyed in the third degree area, meaning that there is numbness and a lack of pain. Intense pain occurs in the edges where the severity fades to second degree.

In assessing severity, it is also important to determine how much of the body has been burned. A helpful rule to keep in mind is the rule of nines. A patient's palm is considered one percent of their surface area. The different body areas of an adult are divided into 9% or multiples of 9% of the body's surface area. Each arm and the head is 9%, each leg, the anterior torso, and the posterior torso are all

18%. The proportion of a child's body is different: 18% for head, anterior torso, and posterior torso, 9 for each arm, and 14% for each leg. Burns are considered critical if they: compromise the airway or cause a loss of function, they result from chemicals or electricity, if they are circumferential, coupled with deformity, or received by children or the elderly. Other indications of severity are based entirely on extent: more the 10% of the body covered by 3rd degree burns, or more than 25% of the body covered by 2nd degree burns. In children and the elderly, this percentage is dropped to 20%.

The responder should be familiar with the nine key steps for treating emergency burn victims, including how this care should be managed for different degrees and classifications. Bandages and dressings should be used to prevent contamination, bleeding, and further trauma to the open area. Standard treatment regimens include high flow supplemental oxygen, cool water, and clean sheets or dry sterile bandages. The responder should also be familiar with the three key questions in determining the severity of the burn, as well as the key factors which allow respiratory assessment.

Part 3: Neck and Facial Injuries

Neck and facial injuries are critical because they bring in concerns regarding airway obstruction, as well as the potential for profuse bleeding and disfiguring scars. These areas include the mouth, throat, nose, eyes, ears, and teeth. In order to treat these injuries effectively, it is important to be familiar with the bones of the face and skull, as well as the connections between throat, nose, and ears, and the anatomy and physiology of the eye. The face and neck contain many veins, so soft tissue injuries in this region generally result in bleeding or bruising. Even a small open wound can produce a large amount of blood, and bruises or hematomas can easily result from closed injuries. Dental injuries can result as well. These can include lacerations to the cheek, frenulum, tongue, gum, or lip, as well as cracked or broken teeth. These injuries may also be caused by foreign objects.

Proper assessment requires an understanding of the major facial bones, as well as attention to both the airway and the anatomy of the specific area injured. Precautions should be taken to avoid contamination, given the high risk of bleeding. The airway should be assessed and managed, and neurological assessment should be made as well. It is important to remove all coverings of the face, neck, and head so that the entire area can be evaluated for airway obstruction, fractures, or bleeding. The responder should be familiar with all proper techniques for fractures, impaled objects, and wounds.

The eyes are a critical area, one of the major senses and vulnerable to a wide range of traumatic injury or medical emergency. The eyes are composed of globes approximately an inch in diameter which contain fluid termed vitreous and aqueous humor. The globe is formed of layers, the outermost being the white sclera, and the outermost is the retina. The retina receives an image that passes through the pupil, the dark portion in the center of the eye, and then through the lens, which focuses the image on the macula of the retina. This image is then received by the optic nerve. The iris is the colored portion surrounding the pupil, which dilates or contracts in response to different light levels. The iris and pupil are covered by a transparent covering termed the cornea. The globes of the eye are set in an orbital socket, surrounded and protected by the bones of the face, and moved and guided by extraocular muscles. In addition, lining the front of the eye and inside of the eyelid is a mucosal layer known as the conjunctiva.

Due to their delicacy and highly complex nature, eyes are prone to a number of medical conditions and forms of trauma. Minor injuries can include slight scrapes to the sclera or irritations of a contact lens. However, injuries can be extremely severe, potentially resulting in the loss of sight in the eye or loss of the eye itself. Saline wash is a form of basic treatment, as is covering or guarding the eye. If the eye has been impaled by a foreign object, it is crucial to stabilize the object until the patient is transferred. With severe eye emergencies, timing is of the utmost importance. The faster the patient can be transported to the receiving hospital and transferred into qualified care, the better the patient outcome will be. The eyes can also be indicators of underlying medical conditions. Anisocoria is a condition in which the pupils are unequal. Though it is a natural condition in some individuals, it can also be a sign of seizure, meningitis, aneurysm, brain tumor, inflammation of the optic nerve, bleeding in the skull, concussion, or direct trauma to the eye.

When the nose is injured, one of the most basic results is epistaxis, or nosebleeds. Also common are swelling of or around the nose, bruising around the eyes, or difficulty breathing through the nose. If the force has been severe, then the cartilage of the nose may be broken, as may be the facial bones in the region. At particular risk are the turbinates, three thin curved shelves of bone in the sides of the nasal cavity. When responding to ear injuries, it is important to understand the physiology of the ear and hearing. Injuries may be sustained to inner, middle, or outer ear, and each has unique complications. In most instances, emergency responders are limited to stabilizing the patient and transporting them to receive treatment from a qualified physician for both intensive assessment and treatment.

The facial area contains a number of different bones, including a portion of the skull, the teeth, the jaw, cheeks, inner bones of the ear, and those that support the nose and surround the eyes. The ear contains the tragus, which is a prominence on the inner side of the external ear, partially closing the passage to the inner ear. Connecting the jaw to the skull is the temporomandibular joint, or TMJ. Fractures to any of these bones results in delicate injuries and potentially involves bleeding or respiratory compromise. One particularly injury to the bones surrounding the eye is known as a blowout fracture. This is a traumatic deformity of the orbital floor or medial wall surrounding the eye. The cheeks themselves are composed of numerous bones. Symptoms of injury to this region can include swelling and involvement of the nerves or muscles. The cheek bones themselves may be misaligned or indented.

Emergency care includes treating impalement, fracture, or bleeding, and stabilizing the injury.

Teeth can be dislodged, broken, or loose, and they can be a source of bleeding or pain. Broken or chipped teeth should be recovered if possible, and handled only by the crown. The gums and mucous membranes of the mouth may also be injured when the teeth have sustained trauma. The responder should be familiar with techniques for responding promptly to fractures or dental trauma.

The neck contains a number of delicate muscles and crucial veins and arteries, as well as the cervical spine and the portion of the spinal cord that it protects. Injuries differ on the depth of the trauma. Superficial injuries are closer to the surface, while arterial or venous levels of injury can interfere with the flow of blood to the brain. Any bleeding in this area should be stopped as soon as possible. The sternocleidomastoid muscles are on the sides of the neck and control the turning of the face from side to side. They connect the sternum and mastoid process, or the bony prominence behind the ears. The neck also contains the upper airway, so trauma can potentially interfere with ventilation. Injury to the seven vertebrae of the cervical spine is also extremely serious. In these instances, remember to stabilize the neck and use the jaw thrust to maintain airway. If the larynx is injured, subcutaneous emphysema, edema, bleeding, and hematoma may result. Emergency treatment is focused on maintaining airway and managing bleeding.

Part 4: Head and Spinal Injuries

The skull and spine house the central nervous system, which is the master controller of all motion, sensation, and bodily function. The spine is composed of 33 bones called vertebrae and arranged into five sections, based on the part of the body and the function they perform. Between each vertebra is a cartilaginous intervertebral disk. The spine houses and protects the spinal cord, as well as functioning structurally to maintain alignment and upright position. The skull itself contains eighteen major bones which form two major structures: the cranium and the face.

Structurally, it is responsible for housing and protecting the brain.

The brain and spine together form the central nervous system, which is surrounded by membranous coverings known as meninges. The meninges are composed of three layers: the dura mater or outermost layer, the arachnoid or central layer, and the pia mater, or inner layer. The peripheral nervous system consists of all of the sensory and motor nerves which run through the rest of the body and direct both involuntary and voluntary functions. The voluntary function of the nervous system is also known as somatic, while the involuntary function is also known as autonomic.

There are three portions to the head: skull, brain, and scalp. Any of these areas can be affected by a head injury, and these fall into two main types. In closed head injuries, the skull is not broken. In open head injuries, the skull is broken and the object penetrates into the brain. Minor injuries can be nothing more than a small bump or superficial abrasion, or far more serious, such as a brain injury, skull fracture, contusion, concussion, hematoma, or laceration. The scalp, just like the face, contains an abundance of veins and capillaries. Lacerations will bleed copiously, and may conceal other head injuries. Watch for the presence of bruising and hematomas as indications of serious injury. If the injury extends into the skull, it may result in an open or closed fracture.

Depending on the mechanism of injury, fractures may come in a number of different forms. They may be linear, meaning that they extend in a line without moving the bone. Depressed skull fractures are visible as dents in the bone of the skull. Diastatic fractures are breaks along and widening of the suture lines. Basilar fractures are breaks in the bone at the base of the skull. They are the most serious type of fracture. Symptoms include bruises around the eyes (raccoon eyes) and behind the ears (battle sign), as well as clear fluid draining from nose and ears due to a tear in the meninges.

If an external force has been significant enough to cause a brain dysfunction, it is known as a traumatic brain injury. The signs can present on an emotional and cognitive level. There are also a variety of types of brain injury, including contusion, concussion, and intracranial pressure. Signs and symptoms include loss of consciousness, apneic episodes, slurred speech, decreased motor function, head pain, vomiting, visual changes, dizziness, and temporary short term amnesia. Amnesia may also be retrograde, which is the loss of older memories, or anterograde, which is the inability to form new memories. Concussions result from an impact to the head which causes the brain to shake within the skull. In these instances, permanent brain damage is not likely. Despite this, concussed patients should still be monitored closely, as a loss of consciousness or apneic episodes may be life-threatening.

Contusions are much more serious, having the potential to produce structural injury to the brain which causes permanent brain damage. They are the result of direct impact, just as in the case of concussion; however, a contusion causes swelling, bleeding, and bruising of the brain tissue. When cerebral edema, known in layman's terms as swelling of the brain, or bleeding inside the skull, also known as intracranial or subarachnoid hemorrhage occurs, the patient experiences increased intracranial pressure. Intracranial pressure may be caused by epidural hematoma, which is swelling outside the meninges surrounding the brain, or subdural hematoma, which is bleeding within the meninges.

Symptoms of intracranial pressure include double vision, pupils that do not respond to light, vomiting, headache, and nausea, confusion about people, places, and time, decreased mental abilities, and increased blood pressure. As the pressure increases, the condition becomes more severe and produces more symptoms. Other injuries to the brain may be non-traumatic, meaning that permanent damage is not likely; however, short term symptoms may be similar to those described for more severe injuries.

One of the most critical steps in emergency treatment for brain trauma patients is to manage the airway. Injury to the spine may be possible, so it is important to use the jaw thrust technique for opening the airway. Only if this is ineffective should other methods be used. The next step after assessing breathing is to check circulation. Check for abnormal speed or strength of the pulse. This will help to determine the type and extent of the injury.

Injuries to the spine itself can be complicated due to the many parts of the spine and spinal cord. These include injuries to the vertebrae, muscles, joints, ligaments, discs, nerves, or spinal cord itself. This often occurs due to axial loading injuries, which result from force applied to the spine through the top of the head. Common signs and symptoms include a loss of sensation or muscle control or pain and tenderness. Patients with a high index of suspicion for spinal injury should be assessed for airway, circulation, and sensory and motor function. Manage airway first, opening it with the jaw thrust technique, and following if necessary with head tilt chin lift, only if necessary and allowed within the scope of practice. Provide assisted ventilation if necessary.

If considering a backboard, cervical collar, vacuum, short board vest, or splint, the spinal area should be evaluated for lacerations or open wounds prior to immobilization. Current best practice requires patients to be assessed according to their presentation prior to the use of immobilization in order to avoid further injury. The responder should be familiar with local protocol to determine whether a cervical collar or backboard is required.

When transferring a patient onto a backboard or packaging them for the ambulance, the four person log roll can be helpful for stabilizing the spine while moving the patient. When preparing for transport, a number of factors must be taken into consideration. These include type of injury, airway, breathing, and circulation status, level of consciousness, geographic location, and patient population. Given the position of the patient and the condition of the spine, the best position for transport may require immobilization, or may be transported in a standing, seated, or supine position. Depending on the severity of the injury and other considerations, ambulance or air transport may be preferable, and, if ambulance transport is selected, it can be operated either without or with lights and sirens. When patients are critical, it is important to reduce on scene time to improve patient outcomes.

If a patient is wearing a helmet, there are special considerations to be taken into account to avoid further injury. The patient should be assessed according to the three general principles designed to protect and maintain central nervous system function: assess airway, bleeding, and level of consciousness. The responder should be familiar with the two-person method for helmet removal, with one person at the shoulders and another at the top of the head. For helmets that include face masks, guards, and pads, the responder should be familiar with the alternative technique, which involves the removal of screws and straps.

Part 5: Chest Injuries

The thorax or chest is the region of the body contained by sternum and ribs. It also contains the lungs, heart, arteries, and blood vessels, key portions of the circulatory and respiratory system. The rib cage connects the vertebral column with the sternum. One half of the chest is known in medical terminology as the hemithorax. Trauma to the thorax can impact the anterior chest wall, as well as to the organs beneath. Intrathoracic pressure can result and the function of the respiratory system can also be compromised. The responder should be familiar with the anatomy and physiology of the respiratory system in order to understand how trauma to the chest wall can interfere with the process of exhalation and inhalation.

Chest injuries can be closed, in which case the chest wall has not been penetrated, or open, in which case a foreign object or bone has pierced the chest wall. Closed chest wounds typically result from blunt force trauma and the symptoms include internal bleeding, damage to the chest wall, ruptured aorta, detached organs, bruising, compromised airway, and pain. Open chest injuries can show symptoms of a compromised airway in addition to bleeding and pain. Common chest injuries include broken ribs or flail chest, which involves ribs broken so badly that they have separated from the remainder of the rib cage. Pneumothorax, or collapsed lung, involves air trapped in the chest, pressing the lung flat and potentially against the heart and other lung. Sucking chest wounds, or holes in the chest wall, are a form of open chest injury. They can potentially pull air into the chest with each breath. Gunshot wounds are another open chest injury which may be encountered in the field.

There are twelve chest injuries described as the "deadly dozen". Six of these are known as the "Lethal Six": airway obstruction, tension pneumothorax, cardiac tamponade, open pneumothorax, massive hemothorax, and flail chest. The others are known as the "Hidden Six": thoracic aortic disruption, tracheobronchial disruption, myocardial contusion, traumatic diaphragmatic tear, esophageal disruption, and pulmonary contusion. The lethal six are immediately life threatening and should be detected during primary assessment. The hidden six are potentially life threatening and should be detected during secondary assessment. The responder should be familiar with signs and symptoms of these injuries so that prompt, appropriate treatment and transport can be provided.

Common symptoms of chest injury include hypoxia, cyanosis, and tachypnea, or abnormally fast breathing, in the case of respiratory compromise. During assessment, special attention should be paid to the physiology of the location which received trauma, as well as pertinent negatives and details regarding special populations. Look for compromise to airway or ventilation, signs and symptoms of collapsed lung, low blood oxygen, abnormally high heart rate, or poor capillary refill. Paradoxical motion, or the tendency of the chest to move inward during inhalation and outward during exhalation, is a sign of flail chest. Hemoptysis, or the coughing up of blood of blood or bloody mucus, is another sign of chest injury.

There are a great number of complications which can arise from trauma to the chest wall and affect the lungs, hear, and large blood vessels. These include pleurisy, or the inflammation of the tissue lining the lungs and rib cage, as well as spontaneous pneumothorax, or the pleural spaces filling with air. Tension pneumothorax is ongoing accumulation of air in the pleural cavity, causing a progressive collapsing of a lung as well as, potentially, tracheal deviation. This occurs when pressure builds up in one side of the chest cavity and the trachea is pushed to one side. Tracheal deviation can be detected by palpating the neck behind and superior to the jugular notch towards the larynx. Deviation occurs on the opposite side of the neck from the side of the chest which has greater pressure. Pneumothorax can be relieved with a chest tube inserted into the pleura, especially when fit with a flutter valve to prevent air from returning into the chest cavity.

Hemothorax, or the collection of blood in the pleural cavity, can also occur. When both pneumothorax and hemothorax occur, the condition is called hemopneumothorax. When these conditions occur, they will create tension in the chest cavity and reduced venous return to the heart. Symptoms include shortness of breath, chest pain, rapid breathing, and rapid heart rate, followed by shock. Similar to these conditions is cardiac tamponade, in which the pericardium, or sac around the heart, fills with fluid. Symptoms include anxiety, restlessness, low blood pressure, weakness, fainting, dizziness, and loss of consciousness, difficulty breathing, rapid breathing, pain radiating from the chest to neck, shoulders, and back. Key signs include visible jugular vein distension (JVD), narrowing pulse pressure, and muffled heart sounds. The pain is often improved by sitting up or leaning forward and made worse by taking deep breaths. Open chest wounds can also result in subcutaneous emphysema, or air trapped under the skin. Symptoms will include crepitus, or a crackling sound in the skin when palpated. Also be aware of signs of cyanosis, absent breath sounds, or cracked ribs.

There are several other injuries which can occur to the chest and the organs within. Myocardial contusions are bruises to the heart, and pulmonary contusions are bruises to the lungs. Depending on the extent of pulmonary contusion, fluid can collect in lung tissues and interfere with gas exchange, causing hypoxia. Commotio cordis is another condition which occurs as a result of a blow over the heart. This is an often lethal disruption of the heart rhythm, commonly occurring in otherwise healthy young male athletes. Treatment involves CPR and defibrillation. Traumatic asphyxia is a rare but serious condition which results from intense chest compression. It is treated with supplemental oxygen, airway support, and bag mask ventilation, as well as IV administration of crystalloid solution to prevent hypovolemia. Possible secondary complications include pneumothorax or hemothorax.

Any bleeding from open chest wounds should be stopped, and the wounds should be dressed with occlusive dressing to prevent blood loss and the entry of air into the chest cavity. The responder should also be prepared to handle minor fractures and contusions, as well as pre-hospital treatment for lacerations of the great vessels. In the event of serious chest injuries, symptom management and rapid transport are vital, especially if surgery is required.

Part 6: Abdominal and Genitourinary Injuries

Injuries to the abdomen and genitals can occur with penetrating force and blunt force trauma. Conditions particular to this region also include evisceration, as well as sexual assault, vaginal bleeding, and trauma to external genitalia. The abdomen contains several organs, including the stomach, liver, pancreas, gallbladder, spleen, small and large intestine, kidneys, and adrenal glands. It contains a membrane known as the peritoneum, which contains all of these organs except for the kidneys, which are in the retroperitoneal space, or the space behind the perineum. The peritoneum also has a double fold which is the site of attachment of the intestine. This is termed the mesentery and is considered a distinct organ. The peritoneum may become inflamed in a condition called peritonitis. The responder should be familiar with the location and function of all of these organs, as well as the quadrant (or quadrants) of the abdomen in which they are contained.

The hollow organs within this space are the stomach, small and large intestine and they are part of the digestive system. Perforations to these organs can cause food and digestive fluids to leak into the abdominal cavity. The solid organs within this system are essential for function of the digestive system as well, so injuries to these organs require prompt attention. Closed abdominal injuries are the result of blunt force trauma to the abdomen. Symptoms of impact to abdominal organs include bruising, inflammation, tenderness, distention, rebound tenderness, which is pain on the removal of pressure, and occasionally referred pain, which is pain at other sites than the affected area. The patient may exhibit abdominal rigidity, an involuntary contraction of the abdominal muscles, or guarding, a voluntary contraction to avoid pain. Another symptom of bleeding in the upper gastrointestinal tract is melena, or dark, tarry stool.

Open abdominal injuries result from penetrating injury and show signs of pain, bleeding, and potentially evisceration, a condition in which organs protrude from an injury in the abdomen. Protocol in dealing with open abdominal injuries depends on the quadrant affected, as this determines the organs which receive trauma. In posterior penetrating abdominal wounds, the organs most likely affected will be retroperitoneal, and the mass of the muscles of the flank (the portion of the back below the ribs and above the hip) will make proper assessment more challenging. Proper treatment depends upon timely assessment, and often include both closed and open trauma. It is important to remember that symptoms that do not at first seem life threatening may have severe complications, so care should be taken to accurately assess all wounds during secondary assessment and reassessment.

It should also be remembered that pediatric patients tend to have weaker abdominal muscles and less fat, meaning that they have less protection from trauma. In addition, children's ribs tend to be more flexible, protecting the ribs from damage but making damage to the internal organs via the ribs more likely. Solid organs are proportionately larger, providing a greater surface area for potential injury. Organ attachments are more elastic, increasing the likelihood of injury due to shearing or tearing. Finally, the bladder extends to the umbilicus, making it more prone to injury as well.

It should be assumed that all abdominal injuries are serious and in need of quick transport to the appropriate trauma center. Open wounds are easier to assess and triage based on severity given that the responder has the necessary level of expertise. Closed wounds cannot be accurately visualized, so they are considered higher risk. Exit wounds should be assessed thoroughly and treated accordingly. With open abdominal injuries, the patient should be examined at back and sides for exit wounds and a dry, sterile dressing applied to all wounds. If the wound is caused by a penetrating object and the object is still in place, then bandages should be placed around it to stabilize it and control bleeding. In the event of evisceration, the wound should be covered by sterile dressings moistened with saline solution and bandaged in place. The patient should also be kept warm and supine to reduce the likelihood of shock.

The genitourinary system is responsible for reproductive function and for excretion of urinary waste. The urinary system is composed of urethra, ureters, urinary bladder, and kidneys. These organs are situated behind the organs of the digestive system. A key organ in this system is the kidney, a solid organ which filters the blood and channels waste materials through the ureters into the bladder. The reproductive system differs in men and women, and each is prone to different injuries based on their structure. Main differences include the fact that the female genitalia are contained within the pelvic cavity with the exception of the vulva, labia, and clitoris, and the male genitalia are outside of the pelvic cavity with the exception of the seminal vesicles and prostate gland.

Potential injuries can occur to the bladder, kidneys, external and internal female genitalia, and external male genitalia. Given the location of some of these organs in the posterior of the abdominal cavity, assessment can be difficult and few external signs or symptoms may show. Common symptoms include nausea, vomiting, diarrhea, hematuria, and hematemesis. Abnormal bladder and bowel habits are another indication. When taking history, the patient should be asked about allergies to environmental triggers or medication. Another important detail is the last intake of fluids and food.

Injury to the bladder can result from penetrating wounds to the lower abdomen, blunt injury when the bladder is fully distended, and sharp bony fragments from a fractured pelvis. In men, injury may come from shearing stress which separates the urethra and bladder, most commonly from motorcycle crashes. In women, pregnancy can cause the uterus to injure the bladder in the second and third trimester. One common symptom is blood in the urine. Patient should be assessed for blood at the urethral opening, or physical signs of trauma to the lower abdomen, pelvis, or perineum. Assessment should focus on signs of shock or the presence of associated injuries. Treatment involves rapid transport, monitoring of vitals, and treatment for shock if necessary.

The kidneys may be damaged by blunt force trauma or penetrating trauma to the flank or through the abdomen. Bruises or lacerations may not be visible on the skin upon inspection. If sufficient blood loss has occurred, then the patient will show signs of shock. Blood in the urine, or hematuria, is also a potential sign of kidney damage. Like bladder injury, proper treatment includes treatment for shock and associated injuries, rapid transport, and close monitoring of the vitals during transport.

Damage to the external male genitalia is not often life threatening, and pain is referred to the lower abdomen. If the penis has been injured, typical treatment involves covering exposed areas with moist sterile compresses and applying pressure with dry sterile gauze dressings to stop the bleeding. If any skin has been avulsed or stripped away, the penis should be wrapped in a soft, sterile moist dressing and moistened with sterile solution. The patient should be transported, and pressure should be applied to control bleeding.

With regard to internal female injuries, the fallopian tubes, ovaries, and uterus are rarely damaged due to their protected location. The exception to this is during pregnancy, where the uterus enlarges and lifts into the abdomen. It is then vulnerable to blunt and penetrating injuries. Signs and symptoms of uterine injury include shock and contractions, and potentially internal bleeding. If it is necessary to transport the patient via a backboard during the third trimester, the uterus should be shifted to the left or the backboard should be tilted to the left to lift the uterus off of the vena cava.

External female genitalia may be injured in a number of ways including rape or sexual assault. It is vital to determine mechanism of injury to see if this is the case. Life threatening injuries should be assessed and handled first. A same sex responder should be provided if possible. The patient should be approached with empathy, care, and patience, and should be assessed for the potential of pregnancy. If bleeding is present, then a pad or sanitary napkin should be applied. Law enforcement should be involved in all cases of rape or sexual assault, and the responder should be familiar with the local protocol for preserving all evidence. It is important to remember that the emotional impact of these events can be just as devastating as the physical impact, so the patient must be handled with great care.

Part 7: Orthopedic Injuries

Orthopedic trauma is injury to the soft tissue, bones, ligaments, joints, and muscles. These can be extremely painful and debilitating, yet they are rarely life threatening. Examples include musculoskeletal injuries and fractures. Proper treatment of orthopedic trauma injuries requires a full understanding of the anatomy and physiology of the muscular and skeletal system and the joints. The skeletal system is composed of bones, which provide structure and containment. They are linked to one another with ligaments. Skeletal muscles are striated muscles which are attached to the skeleton and both support the skeletal system and permit motion across joints. The ends of bones that form joints are covered with a smooth white layer of tissue called articular cartilage. It allows bones to slide against one another with little friction.

The skeletal muscles form the greatest bulk of muscle in the body. The other two types of muscle are smooth muscle, which is linked to the digestive system and circulatory system, and cardiac muscle, which forms the heart tissue. Muscles are innervated by the peripheral nervous system. This is a network of nerves which extend from the central nervous system to the muscles and sensory nerves and organs. Sensory nerves relay sensory information to the central nervous system, while motor nerves relay impulses to motion from the central nervous system to the voluntary muscles of the musculoskeletal system and the involuntary muscles of the digestive and circulatory systems.

The five different forms of orthopedic injury are strains, sprains, dislocations, fractures, and amputations. The zone of injury with musculoskeletal injuries is the area of soft tissue damage surrounding the injury. Dislocations are displacements of the bone ends and damage to the connecting ligaments. If the joint is incompletely dislocated, it is termed a subluxation. Dislocated joints should be splinted in the position in which they are found. Sprains are partial or temporary separation of the bone ends with partial tearing or stretching of the joining ligaments. Symptoms include ecchymosis, point tenderness, and swelling. Strains are stretching or tearing to the muscle. Signs of a strain include bruising, swelling, and pain.

Amputations are the removal of a limb or portion of a limb. Patients should be treated first for blood loss and shock, and the wound should be covered with sterile pads and bandages, or, if necessary, a tourniquet should be applied. If the limb is recovered, is should be placed in sterile dressings and within a plastic bag. The limb should be cooled, but should not be allowed to contact ice directly.

Fractures are breaks in the continuity of the bone. Displaced fractures result in a deformity, or a condition in which the bones are out of their proper position. A reduced joint or fracture is one that has been set back in place after displacement. Non-displaced fractures are simple cracks. Crepitus, point tenderness, and false motion, the movement of a limb where there is no joint, are some of the most reliable indicators of an underlying factor. Other indicators include guarding, swelling, bruising, exposed fragments, and deformity. If the fracture is open, or exposed, then the skin covering the fracture is no longer intact. Complications specifically related to open fractures include long-term disability and deformity.

It is important to understand the mechanism of injury to properly treat an orthopedic injury. The responder should be familiar with the four mechanisms of injury for orthopedic trauma injuries. Responders should also be familiar with the eight types of fractures. Additional symptoms include angulation, rotation, or shortening of the limb. Complications can result from the trauma, and include damage to nerves, arteries and blood vessels as well as bleeding. Musculoskeletal injuries should be splinted to prevent further injury, unless patient transport is of higher priority. It should also be remembered that assessment should take into account other signs and symptoms beyond the orthopedic injury to ensure that all necessary life-preserving measures have been taken. During patient assessment, the musculoskeletal grading system should be used to determine type and severity of the injury. This system evaluates swelling, tenderness, and the limitation of motion.

When treating musculoskeletal injuries, begin with airway, breathing, and circulation. In the case of catastrophic bleeding, sterile dressing should be used to control the bleeding before attempting resuscitation. Sterile dressing should be used to control. The patient should be assessed for sensory and motor function, as well as for distal to pulses. This should be done before and after splinting an injury. The injury should be splinted, treated for swelling, and stabilized prior to transport. The most important consideration is to avoid or reduce any further injury. This requires the use of an appropriate splint and avoiding the compression of tissue, blood vessels, and nerves. Another important consideration is compartment syndrome, which is the prevention of blood flow due to swelling. Compartment syndrome requires prompt transport to prevent further damage to the tissue. The responder should be familiar with the different types of splints and the conditions in which each is used.

Treatments for shoulder dislocations and fractures include applying a sling and swathe.

This is often done using triangular bandages. The sling and swathe is designed to support the arm and keep it close to the body and is used for injuries where moving the shoulder could cause harm.

Part 8: Environmental Emergencies

There are several different forms of environmental emergency. Exposure can happen in climates of extreme heat or cold. Either extreme temperature can challenge the body's homeostasis, it's capacity to regulate it's function within the necessary levels. An individual's capability to tolerate these temperatures depends on nutrition and hydration levels, environmental impact, age, and physical condition. The body requires a core temperature of 95 degrees or higher before hypothermia sets in. When it is exposed to cold beyond certain levels, it is no longer capable of self-regulating body temperature. After continued exposure, the cold can impact body system and organ functions. This is known as hypothermia. Exposure of only a part of the body to cold can cause a local cold injury. If this extends only to the level of the skin, it is known as frostnip or trench foot. Cell damage occurs if the cold extends to deeper levels, leaving the skin frozen, firm, or waxy. This is known as frostbite, and it can leave the tissue cyanotic, mottled, or blistered.

The responders should first wear personal protective equipment to limit their exposure. Assessment follows the typical protocol, and, when it can be done safely, should be transferred to an indoor or sheltered environment. The patient should not be forced to walk. Wet clothing should be removed and replaced with dry blankets. Frostbite should be covered with thick sterile cotton gauze. The responder should not massage the affected area or subject it to friction. The patient should not be allowed to smoke or ingest simulants. Responders should be familiar with the characteristics of systemic hypothermia, and patients should be transferred to the appropriate center if the exposure is significant.

Similarly, if a patient is exposed to heat beyond their capacity to self-regulate, they can suffer hyperthermia. A patient's capacity to self-regulate their temperature is a factor of their physical condition, medical conditions, substances, the level of exercise, and the environmental conditions. The core temperature of the body must be maintained below 101 degrees. If it rises above these temperatures, the patient will experience symptoms of heat stroke, heat exhaustion, or heat cramps, or any combination thereof. Heat cramps are muscular spasms causes by excess heat and insufficient fluids or electrolytes. Severe dehydration can reduce in a loss of turgor or elasticity to the skin.

Signs of heat exhaustion include extreme sweating, lightheadedness, headache, and fatigue. Proper treatment is rehydration, rest, and cooling. If heat exhaustion proceeds further, it will become heat stroke. Signs include hot, flushed skin, and the perspiration will cease. If untreated, heat stroke will progress to seizures and unresponsiveness, and, eventually, brain damage or death.

When encountering patients with heat exposure, responders must first limit their exposure with proper personal protective equipment. Next, the scene should be sized up and the mechanism of injury should be determined. Skin assessment should be made to determine temperature, moisture, turgor, and condition. The patient should be moved to a cooler location or into the shade, and the skin should be dampened or cooled with a fan. Consider removing their clothing. Treatments for heat emergencies also include placing ice packs under the patient's armpits, neck and groin to help reduce body temperature.

Another form of environmental injury is drowning or injuries sustained while diving. Even experienced divers and swimmers can drown, and drowning can occur even in shallow water. The responder should be familiar with the mechanism of drowning and the common emergencies that occur when diving, including resuscitation efforts, recovery techniques, and the potential for spinal injuries. Assessment of the scene includes water temperature, water purity, and submersion timeframe. One challenge this this is that the responder is often unable to get information about length of exposure or the nature of the incident itself. The EMT should be familiar with signs and symptoms of drowning, as well as complications introduced by drug and alcohol usage, medication, and additional injuries.

Typical protocol should be followed in the assessment of diving emergencies, near drowning, and drowning. This begins with scene size up and MOI, taking into consideration all hazards of the environment and details offered regarding the nature of the incident. In assessment, look for underlying causes and related injuries. If spinal injury is suspected, the spine should be immobilized while checking airway, breathing, and circulation. This should be performed prior to removing the victim from the water. The patient should be assessed for symptoms and signs of breath-holding syncope, as well as bleeding injuries or critical head injuries. Treatment includes supplemental oxygen. Patients should be assessed for decompression illness, pneumothorax, and any other conditions which require immediate care. Pediatric patients should be stabilized after treatment, even if they appear to be completely stable.

The key to reducing the likelihood of drowning and diving accidents is prevention. Responders can share water safety information with the public to aid prevention. This includes the use of fences around pools, the buddy system when swimming, and ensuring trained lifeguards are present in public swimming areas. Public swimming areas should also contain working phones and AEDs. Finally, drug and alcohol use should be avoided when swimming or bathing.

Another environmental danger is high altitude. At high altitudes, air pressure and partial pressure of oxygen are lower than at sea level. When pressure is different between the environment and the tissues and cavities inside of the body, the condition is known as dysbarism. Dysbarism injury can cause problems in both the central nervous system and pulmonary system. High-Altitude Pulmonary Edema, or HAPE, occurs when fluid fills the lungs in high altitude. High-Altitude

Cerebral Edema, or HACE, occurs when the brain swells with fluid at high altitudes. Altitude sickness is hypoxia resulting from lower partial pressure of oxygen at higher altitudes. Symptoms of these conditions include fatigue and weakness, difficulty sleeping, lightheadedness, dizziness, vomiting, nausea and anorexia. The principle symptom will be a headache. Primary treatment include slowly lowering altitude, or, if necessary, providing a portable hyperbaric chamber. The responder should be aware of the medications used for acclimatization and within the scope of practice.

Another environmental hazard is lightning. Patients may be struck directly or indirectly, most often in open areas. The resulting injury is produced by heat, electricity, and mechanical energy. The first step is to assess the hazards and ensure that the patients and responders are in a safe area. The electrical shock of a lightning strike often causes asystole or cardiac dysrhythmias that spontaneously resolve. Reverse triage should be performed for multiple lightning strike patients, meaning that those without breathing and circulation should receive medical attention first. Lightning injuries will often impact tissues as well as the nervous and cardiovascular systems, and the severity of lightning strikes are classed in categories of mild, medium, and severe. Patients should be assessed for exit and entry wounds. After resuscitation and assessment, the patient should be transported and inspected by a physician for a wide range of potential complications.

Toxins and venoms from animal and insect bites and stings can also produce a wide range of severe medical conditions. These include bites and stings from snakes, scorpions, ticks, ants, yellow jackets, wasps, bees, and spiders. Even when the stings or bites themselves are not venomous, there is the potential for allergic reaction, ranging from mild, such as urticaria or hives, to life-threatening anaphylaxis. Those that do inject venom often require the prompt use of an antivenin in treatment. Given the wide range of different venomous creatures, it is important for the responder to understand the venomous creatures in their area, as well as the signs and symptoms of their bites and stings.

Stings from toxic marine animals are particularly serious. Some of the more common creatures are jellyfish, also known as coelenterates, sting rays, and sea urchins. Each requires a different form of treatment and comes in a wide range of different severities. As with stings from land creatures and insects, allergic reaction is a potential complication. Stings from coelenterates generally require that the patient is removed from the water, and the stung area is scraped with a stiff object such as a credit card to remove the microscopic barbs. Common symptoms of these stings include headaches, dizziness, redness, and pain at the site of the sting. Urchin and stingray stings can be treated with vinegar soaks or hot water. As with land creatures, responders should be familiar with the marine hazards native to their area, as well as signs and symptoms and the proper methods of treatment.

Part 9: Shock

Shock is a complication of many different medical conditions. It is an acute circulatory condition resulting from inadequate perfusion of the tissues. Essentially, the blood pressure is too low to meet the oxygen demands of tissues and organs. Hypoperfusion provides insufficient oxygen, often resulting from lower pulse pressure or a constriction of blood vessels. Shock can also result from fluid loss due to spinal cord injury, septicemia, vomiting, or diarrhea. Other potential causes include pulmonary embolism or cardiac arrest.

Each different type of shock requires treatment based on the underlying physiological cause. Distributive shock results from excessive vasodilation and impaired blood flow. The most common form of this is septic shock. Hypovolemic shock results from a lower blood volume, and it is the most common form of shock. Primary treatment includes administering intravenous isotonic crystalloid solution. Cardiogenic or obstructive shock occurs when the heart pumps an insufficient volume of blood or when perfusion to the heart is obstructed. Neurogenic shock is a result of nervous system injury leading to excessive peripheral vasodilation. Psychogenic shock is the result of intense emotion or stress which causes vasodilation and a drop in blood pressure. Anaphylactic shock is vasodilation and bronchial constriction as a result of a severe allergic reaction. The responder should be familiar with the different forms of shock and the appropriate method for treating each, as proper treatment relies on the proper diagnosis of the underlying cause.

There are three stages of shock: compensated, decompensated, and irreversible. The first stage, compensated shock, results in increased heart rate, constriction of the blood vessels, and the tendency of the kidney to retain fluid. Aggressive treatment is often capable of slowing the development of decompensated shock, however, shock can be difficult to detect as it has few symptoms. When shock moves on to the second stage decompensated shock, the compensation methods begin to fail. During decompensated shock the blood pressure will begin to fall, (often systolic of 90 mm HG or lower for adults) the patient may have decreased mental status and dilated pupils. The organs, tissues and brain become significantly deprived of oxygen. One symptom of cerebral deprivation of oxygen is confusion and disorientation. Without treatment, the patient will deteriorate into the third stage, irreversible shock. The deprivation of oxygen then leads to cell damage and organ failure. The endpoint of this stage is death.

The primary complaint of the patient will often not be shock. However it is a serious condition that requires immediate treatment. Responders should assess heart rate and vitals for signs and should be familiar with other key identifiers. It should be remembered that the signs of each form of shock will differ and provide guidance for necessary treatment. Emergency care requires focused triage to determine the most life-threatening symptoms and address them promptly. Once again, the underlying condition must be treated to effectively handle the specific form for shock exhibited by your patient such as stopping bleeding. Treatment also includes keeping the patient warm with legs raised and head down to improve blood flow to the brain as well as administering supplemental oxygen.

This completes the EMT study guide for the NREMT examination. We wish you the best in your new and rewarding career as an EMT!

Printed in the USA
CPSIA information can be obtained
at www.ICGtesting.com
LVHW091032120724
785206LV00009B/100